THE BIG BOOK OF LIFE SKILLS FOR KIDS

Books by Sandy Silverthorne

THE BIG BOOK OF
LIFE
SKILLS
FOR KIDS

LEARN TO PACK YOUR LUNCH, TO TALK WITH GOD,
AND 99 OTHER THINGS EVERYONE SHOULD KNOW

SANDY SILVERTHORNE

Revell

a division of Baker Publishing Group
Grand Rapids, Michigan

© 2025 by Sandy Silverthorne

Published by Revell
a division of Baker Publishing Group
Grand Rapids, Michigan
RevellBooks.com

Printed in the United States of America

Library of Congress Cataloging-in-Publication Data
Names: Silverthorne, Sandy, 1951– author.
Title: The big book of life skills for kids : learn to pack your lunch, talk with God, and 99 other things everyone should know / Sandy Silverthorne.
Description: Grand Rapids, Michigan : Revell, a division of Baker Publishing Group, [2025] | Audience: Ages 6–8
Identifiers: LCCN 2024033234 | ISBN 9780800745448 (paper) | ISBN 9780800746858 (casebound) | ISBN 9781493448746 (ebook)
Subjects: LCSH: Christian children—Conduct of life—Juvenile literature.
Classification: LCC BV4571.3 .S548 2025 | DDC 242/.62—dc23/eng/20241115
LC record available at https://lccn.loc.gov/2024033234

Cover design by Gayle Raymer
Cover illustration by Sandy Silverthorne

The author is represented by WordServe Literary Group, www.wordserve literary.com.

Baker Publishing Group publications use paper produced from sustainable forestry practices and postconsumer waste whenever possible.

25 26 27 28 29 30 31   7 6 5 4 3 2 1

To Vicki:
You're my love, my best friend, and my biggest encourager.
I'm so thankful I get to experience God's goodness
throughout life with you.

To Christy:
What a gift you are to me and to so many others.
It's fun to see how God is using and expanding your gifts
to bless so many people.

To Nick Harrison:
I have you to thank for the original idea for this book.
Thank you! God has used you to open so many doors for me,
and for that I'm truly grateful.

Contents

Contents

Contents

Contents

Contents

Introduction

How do I make friends? How do I order food in a restaurant? Can I really calm myself down when I get upset? And can I get to know God? Really? Is that even possible?

Being a kid can be a fun, new, and exciting adventure every day. But sometimes it can be downright confusing. There are so many questions and things to learn all the time: How do I ride a bike? How do I cook some simple meals? And even, How can I learn to tell a good joke?

In this book you'll learn all sorts of important things that every kid should know. Like how to join a team, keep your room clean, or shop for groceries. And how to make good decisions, pack your suitcase for a sleepover, plant a garden, or handle your money.

So, get ready to be the smartest kid in the room. Or at least the most interesting.

There are a couple ways you can use this book. You might just pick it up and read the whole thing through like you do with most books.

Or you might go to the table of contents and choose one or two things that you really want to know and read them first.

Interested in learning how to care for your pet? Or how to be found or do better with your schoolwork? Check out chapters 32, 71, and 77.

Now, of course, no book can answer every single question you might have about growing up. But here's the good news: This book will also help you get to know the One who does have all the answers. It's God! He loves you so much, and He's just waiting for you to come to Him for answers to all the questions—BIG and small—that you might have about growing up in this wonderful world He's created.

So, get ready! And have fun learning all kinds of new things!

If you have more questions or want to go deeper into any of the subjects, just let me know at SandySilverthorneBooks.com.

Have a Thankful Attitude

This sounds pretty easy, doesn't it? I mean, you say thank you when someone gives you a present or when they pass the rice at the dinner table. But did you know that by being thankful, you're actually making your brain work better? And that being thankful even makes you happier? Look around you. Can you think of some things to be thankful for? Things like your dog or your cat, your house, the fact that you can read! Or ride a bike. Are you thankful for your brother or sister? Okay, maybe not right this minute but most of the time?

By being thankful, you're training your brain to see the good stuff going on all around you. We all know how easy it is to focus on the bad stuff in life, but when you find things to be thankful for, your attitude will change and your mood can even get better. That might be one reason God wants us to be thankful all the time! (Check out 1 Thess. 5:18 in the Bible.)

Try it for a week. You might list five things you're thankful for right when you wake up or maybe at the end of the day when you're about to go to sleep. Go ahead, try it! You might see a difference in your mood right away!

List five things you're thankful for right now:

Learn How to Make Friends

Some people seem to make friends easily. In fact, it's almost like people come searching for them! They might be really gifted in athletics, or they might be musical or even really funny, so they always seem to be surrounded by people who want to be their friend. But if you're like most kids, you might find it hard to make friends. You might be at a new school, or maybe you're a little shy and nervous about going up to somebody and saying, "Hi, you wanna be my friend?" Most people have trouble making new friends, but never fear! Here are some ideas on how to start to develop good friendships:

1. The first and most important way to make a friend is by being a friend yourself! That means not making everything about you. Don't just talk all the time. Don't make people always do things the way you want to do them. Show that you care about them. Remember their birthday. Call them up once in a while. If they ask you to help them with something, help them out if you can. Show yourself to be a good friend to them.

2. One way to make some friends, especially if you're at a new school, is to find a group and join it. A sports team like soccer, volleyball, or baseball might be just the way for you to get to know kids who are interested

in the same things you are. Or you might join a music group, try out for a play, or get involved in the science fair, chess club, or math fair. That's a great way to meet people.

3. When you're in a class or group activity, or even waiting for the school bus, and you see a kid you'd like to get to know, go on over and introduce yourself. You might say something like "Hi, my name is _____ (don't say "blank"—use your real name). I like your backpack," or "Cool T-shirt. Did you get it in New York City?" (Only say this if their T-shirt has something about New York City on it.)

4. Ask them questions. Everybody likes to tell you their story. "Are you new at school?" "What kinds of things do you like to do?" "Seen any good movies lately?" "Do you have any brothers or sisters?" "Do they annoy you?" That kind of thing.

5. Step out. Don't always wait for the other person to invite you to do something. If you'd like them to come over after school sometime or sit with you at lunch, let them know. And if they say no, don't take it too personally. They may have other things to do at that time. But if they say no every time, you might need to look for another good friend.

Write down some questions you might like to ask someone when you meet them for the first time.

3 Pack Your Own Lunch for School

As you get a little older, you might want to start making your own lunch for school. After all, don't you want to give your mom or dad a little break from all they do for you? Plus, making your own lunch gives you the chance to be creative and put stuff in there you really want. But make sure you include some healthy food. As tempting as it is, don't pack your lunch with just cupcakes, cookies, and candy!

Here are some things you might want to include in a healthy lunch:

A sandwich—This could be peanut butter and jelly or honey, tuna fish, or some kind of lunch meat, like bologna, ham, or turkey. For a lunch meat sandwich, get a couple pieces of bread. Spread some mayonnaise on the bread. If you don't like mayonnaise, try some mustard. You might add a slice of cheese, then your turkey, bologna, or ham. Place some lettuce on there to add some crunch. Then put your top piece of bread on and maybe cut it down the middle. A perfect sandwich!

Have you ever tried a peanut butter and *banana* sandwich? Spread peanut butter on bread,

add sliced banana, and place the other slice of bread on top. You'll either love it or hate it.

Sides—These could be potato chips, corn chips, or those cheesy things that turn your fingers all orange as you eat them. Or try some cut-up or baby carrots or broccoli pieces as a healthy side to go with your sandwich.

Dessert—Of course, this is the most fun part of your meal. Stick in a cupcake or a couple cookies. Maybe a fruit-flavored snack. But make sure you always eat your sandwich and sides first. If you eat dessert first, you might forget to eat your sandwich and sides.

Fruit—Top off your excellent hand-packed lunch with a piece of fruit. An apple, orange, banana, or some grapes should do the trick. Rinse them off with water (not the banana), then dry them and stick them in your lunch bag or box. Delicious!

Bread

Lettuce

Lunch meat

Cheese

Bread II

Drink—Make sure you add a cool, refreshing drink in there too. Bottled water, a thermos of juice, or lemonade will top off your lunch perfectly.

If you put all these things inside your lunch, you'll feel good and full of energy for the rest of the day.

Bonus Tip: If you always seem to be in a rush in the morning, why not make your lunch the night before? Get all your pieces together, put them in your lunch box or paper bag, and stick it in the fridge. Then the next morning, you can grab it quick, just as you run out the door.

4 Keep Clean (and Don't Stink!)

When you're a kid, you probably don't care that much about keeping clean. I mean, the important things in your life are playing hard, winning the game, and maybe even getting a little dirty in the process. But there are times—and school is one of them—when you want to be clean and smell good. So, how do you do that?

It's easy. At least every other day—like maybe Monday, Wednesday, and Friday—hop into the shower and clean up. You'll look better, feel better, and yes, you'll even smell better.

Here's how it works:

1. Turn on the shower, let it warm up (not too hot), and get in and rinse your body off.
2. Wash with soap—yes, *use* the soap or body wash—and wash from your face all the way down to your toes.

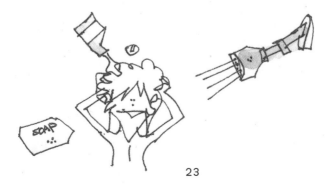

Then rinse the soap off, and there you have it! At least two or three times a week, also wash your hair with shampoo. Rinse all the shampoo out really well, too, or your hair will be all yucky and greasy.

3. Get out and towel off.
4. Then put on some clean clothes, not that stinky T-shirt you've been wearing since last August. And that's it! Simple, huh?

And now you're ready for school! Unless, of course, you shower at night. In *that* case, you'll be ready for bed!

Keeping clean makes you look and smell better, but it's also a way to keep healthy. So, get in the habit of showering at least three times a week, and you (and everyone around you) will be happy!

Also remember, part of keeping clean is brushing your teeth at least twice a day. It's pretty easy. Just grab your toothbrush, put toothpaste on it, and brush for two minutes. Rinse with some water afterward, and your mouth will feel really clean! There are even phone apps that will help you brush correctly.

5 Eat Lunch with the New Kid

Think about it. Have you ever *been* the new kid in school? You don't know anybody. You might feel kind of lost and alone, trying to figure out how things work. That first day can be really tough!

And who knows why they're new? Maybe they've had to move for some reason or other. Or it might be that their mom or dad got a new job. Or maybe their parents got divorced. Or maybe they were bullied at their old school. Doesn't really matter *why* they moved. The first day or two at a new school can be scary. Put yourself in their place for a second. They might feel nervous, awkward, and even a little lonely.

Now, I get that it's hard for most of us to go up to a kid we don't know and start talking. So, what should you do?

Here's an idea: Go over and ask them to sit with you at lunch. You might be the best thing that's happened to them all day! Ask them some questions to get to know them.

Try these:

1. "Hi, I'm _____ [fill in the blank]. What's your name? Are you new here?"
2. "Where did you move from?"
3. "So, what kinds of things do you like? Sports? Reading? Dogs? Movies?"

Then go ahead and tell them the kinds of things you like.

You might even let them know about how things work in your school. Who's who, how classes work, and after-school activities. And if you get the chance, introduce them to some of the kids you know.

You might make their first day at the new school awesome, and you might just make a new best friend. Eat lunch with the new kid!

6 Be Honest

You want your friends and family members to tell you the truth, don't you? Of course. And, naturally, they want you to do the same thing. Sometimes it's hard to tell the truth, though, isn't it? Especially when you think you might get in trouble for something. Also, sometimes we tell lies because we want to look good to someone.

But here's something to think about: Almost every time we tell a lie or are dishonest, it's because we're afraid of something. You might be afraid you're going to get in trouble, so you lie about something that happened. Or you're afraid someone won't like you, so you make up a story about yourself or your family that makes you sound important, hoping the other person will think you're pretty cool.

But if you do this for a while, people might start to figure out you're not telling the truth, and then something bad happens. They stop believing what you say. They stop trusting you. And you don't want that to happen.

Remember, everyone makes mistakes, and part of growing up is learning to admit when you did something wrong. Most of the time, your parents and the people around you would rather you tell the truth than hide a mistake you made.

And if you feel like you need to lie to impress someone in your life, you might want to think about why that's so important to you. If they can't be your friend just as you are, maybe they're not going to be that good a friend after all.

Throughout this book, we'll have several "Talk It Over" sections, where you'll get a chance to share your thoughts with your mom or dad or a small group. Just go through the questions and answer honestly. Remember, there are no wrong answers. Just be yourself and share what you think.

1. Have you ever had somebody lie to you? How did it feel?

2. Have you ever been tempted to lie to someone else? What was going on?

3. If you were ever less than truthful with someone, were you afraid of something? Maybe getting in trouble or not being accepted? Talk about it. How did you feel afterward?

# Practice Makes Perfect

Is there something you'd like to do really well?

Shoot a three-pointer?
Draw an amazing picture?
Play the guitar?
Write stories?
Become an awesome singer?

You can do any of these things, but you'll need to do one thing first—practice! Nobody can shoot a three-pointer the

first time they pick up a basketball. Nobody learns to play the guitar the first day, and learning to draw takes lots of time—and practice. But the good news is that with almost anything, the more you practice, the better you'll get at whatever you're trying to learn.

Do you want to cook an amazing dinner of salmon, potatoes, and salad? That's going to take some practice. So is learning the piano, tackling a new sport, or getting good in science or math.

Here are a few things to remember as you practice:

1. *Start small.* Get real about what you want to do and when. For example, if you want to learn how to play the guitar, start by practicing just a few chords. Work on it for about fifteen minutes a day to begin with. Start small.

2. *Be patient!* As you practice doing something new, you're going to have great days when everything goes smoothly and other days when . . . not so much. Be patient with yourself. Realize that any good thing you want to learn is going to take some time.

3. *Ask for some help.* You might find an older brother or sister, your mom or dad, or even a coach who can help you get better at whatever it is you're trying to learn. And who knows? Someday soon, you might be the one who's helping another kid learn!

4. *Stick with it!* Whatever it is you're wanting to get better at, don't give up! Even on those frustrating days when it feels like you're getting nowhere. Realize that every day, every time you're working on this new skill—even if you can't see it yet—you're getting better. Keep at it.

Even for just five minutes a day. Whether it's a sport, the piano, or understanding math or science, you'll soon start to see progress, and after a while you'll be a pro!

Join a Team

A great way to meet new friends, get some exercise, and have a lot of fun is to join a team. Do you like soccer? Baseball? Swimming? Track? There are a lot of sports out there, and kids like you can get the chance to play almost all of them! You might be a pro at basketball, or you might never have even seen one, but that doesn't matter. Teams are all about learning and becoming the best you can be. So, if this sounds like fun to you, here are a few tips for making the team:

1. First, find out what team sports are available for kids your age. Certain sports, like tackle football, require you to be a certain age to play. See if there are soccer, basketball, or volleyball teams in your area for kids your age. Sometimes they'll put up ads around your school to let kids know when they're holding tryouts. Find out how you can sign up and if it costs anything. Usually, your parents can sign you up online.

2. Make sure you can attend the practices and games. If they're at a time when you're already busy, you might have to wait till next season to try out for that team.

3. Most teams hold a tryout to see where you are in your skills. Don't worry, the coaches just want to see how their team is shaping up. Especially in the early grades.

They're there to help you learn. So, show up, do your best, and have a great attitude.

4. If there are papers your parents need to sign or if you need certain shoes or uniforms, make sure you have that all taken care of before the first practice. This shows the coaches that you're responsible and trustworthy.

5. Control the stuff you can control. That simply means that even if you're not the fastest or most talented player out there, you can always show up on time, listen to instructions, and follow directions. Lots of pro athletes work harder than anyone else on the team, get better and better, and end up playing in the Super Bowl!

6. Have fun!

Team sports are a great way to make friends, learn new skills, and create some fun memories.

DID YOU KNOW?

Popsicles were invented by accident. One day, back in 1905, an eleven-year-old kid named Frank Epperson accidentally left his drink out on his front porch with the stir stick in it. It was cold when he got up the next morning, and the drink had frozen with the stick in it! He'd created the first popsicle!

Take Care of Yourself, Part 1

Eat Right!

What's your favorite thing to eat? Hamburgers? Pizza? Cookies? Fruit? Ice cream? It's fun to eat stuff that tastes really good, like donuts, cupcakes, and desserts, every once in a while. But in order to grow up strong and healthy, it's important to eat the good stuff too.

Did you know that kids like you should eat at least five servings of fruits and vegetables a day? And if you can, try to eat even more. The good news is there are lots of fun and tasty ways to enjoy the stuff that's good for you. You might throw some spinach or kale into a berry smoothie for breakfast. Or instead of potato chips with your sandwich at lunch, try five or six baby carrots. And how about some sliced apples with peanut butter after dinner for a sweet and good-for-you dessert? Or you can make frozen fruit popsicles yourself. I'll share the recipe with you in chapter 15.

If you want to grow up healthy and have plenty of energy for school or for play, make sure you eat plenty of protein too. One or two eggs in the morning, a tuna sandwich for lunch, and maybe some chicken strips for dinner will give you the right amount of protein your body needs. Protein helps your body grow, and it gives you lots of energy for all the stuff you're doing throughout the day.

It's okay to enjoy some ice cream and sweets occasionally, but if you want to help your body grow in a smart and healthy way, make sure you're eating plenty of good-for-you foods too.

Here are some good-for-you foods you should try to include in your diet:

Yogurt—This can be a sweet, smooth after-school treat or dessert after dinner.

Berries—Try adding strawberries, blueberries, raspberries, or blackberries to your cereal.

Avocado—This is good on toast or squished up to make guacamole.

Eggs—Scrambled, fried, or poached—they're always a good way to start the day.

Beans—These are great for protein to give you energy.

Milk—Enjoy a cold glass of 1% or 2% milk.

Vegetables—Tomatoes, broccoli, peas, green beans—you get the idea.

Take Care of Yourself, Part 2

Get Moving!

What's the next tip to help you take care of yourself and keep healthy and growing? Exercise, of course. Now, exercise doesn't mean you've got to do a hundred push-ups or run five miles every day. There are lots of fun ways to exercise, some of which you might be doing already! Let's look at some enjoyable ways to get off the couch and get moving:

1. Ride your bike. If you're going over to a friend's house or even going to school and it's not too far, why not think about riding your bike? It's a great, easy, and fun way to get some exercise without even realizing it. If you don't know how to ride a bike yet, I've got some tips in chapter 87.

2. Play basketball, kickball, or softball with your friends in the neighborhood. Sure, if you can try out for a basketball or soccer or baseball team, you should do it. But if there's not a team available, why not gather a few friends and play in your driveway? Playing basketball for thirty minutes gives you the same amount of exercise as a PE class.

3. Take the dog for a walk. If you keep a quick pace, going for a walk is a great way to get out and get your blood circulating. You and your dog will both feel great after a walk around the block.

You might be thinking, *What if it's raining or snowing and I can't go outside to exercise?* Well, here are some ideas for easy and fun activities you can do indoors:

- Jumping jacks
- Dancing to fun music
- Balancing on one foot
- Follow-the-leader (take turns picking movements)
- Hopscotch (make your hopscotch by placing tape on the floor)
- Blowing up a balloon and keeping it from touching the ground
- Crab-walking or bear-crawling races with your brother or sister
- Jump rope—be careful though; don't hit any furniture

See? Getting a little exercise every day can be really easy and really fun!

Take Care of Yourself, Part 3

Go to Sleep!

One of the best (and easiest!) ways to take care of yourself is by getting enough sleep. Even though you may feel like you've got enough energy to keep going all day and all night, kids actually need more sleep than you think. Adults usually need around seven or eight hours of sleep to feel good and stay healthy. But, believe it or not, kids need somewhere between nine and twelve hours of sleep a night!

Here's how that works: Let's say you need to get up at seven to get ready for school every morning. So, if you're going to get twelve hours of sleep, when should you go to bed?

Seven o'clock at night, right? See? Easy! So, how much sleep do *you* need?

The best way to figure that out is to see how you feel during the daytime. If you feel tired all the time (and you're eating well and getting good exercise), then you might need some extra sleep. Try going to bed a little earlier and see if you feel better the next day. It might take a little while for your body to get used to your new sleep schedule, but once it does, you'll feel much better, be more awake, and have more energy than before.

Believe it or not, getting enough sleep will also help you do better in school because you'll be able to concentrate and remember things too. Getting the right amount of sleep will also help you in your sports and after-school activities.

Here are a few tips to help you go to sleep at night:

Try taking a bath or shower before bed. This helps your body calm down and get ready to sleep.

Turn your lights down so your room isn't too bright before you go to bed. Use just one or two lamps. Less light tells your body that it's nighttime and time to unwind.

Turn off screens. Turn off your computer, your TV, and even your phone, if you have one, at least an hour before you go to bed. The blue light from all those screens tells your body it's daytime and time to wake up. You definitely don't want that going on when you're getting ready for bed.

Read a book in bed. Not on a screen but a real paper book. Reading often makes you drowsy and ready to sleep.

And if you have a cell phone, put it away when you go to bed, or at least put it across the room. Studies have shown that having your phone near you at night interrupts your sleep.

If you do these things every night, it's like you're telling your body, "Okay, it's getting late; we're going to relax and go to sleep soon."

Taking Care of Yourself

Three ways to take care of yourself and grow up strong and healthy are eating right, exercising, and getting plenty of sleep. See if you can find the words from the list below in the word search. They might go across, up, or down!

```
U  H  E  X  R  D  F  R  U  I  T  S  Q
L  Q  C  G  A  S  P  O  R  T  S  W  X
I  H  F  B  W  A  L  K  O  U  X  I  B
T  G  E  Y  D  K  A  E  J  D  N  M  R
I  D  C  A  M  S  Y  E  E  O  C  U  E
Y  B  I  I  L  B  Y  S  N  P  M  E  A
G  E  P  N  Q  T  I  T  F  V  B  A  K
C  D  L  U  N  C  H  R  P  T  E  R  F
S  T  T  Y  R  E  P  Y  S  E  Y  Y  A
T  I  A  E  K  I  R  G  S  X  L  M  S
X  M  X  G  I  C  A  M  U  T  A  L  T
V  E  G  E  T  A  B  L  E  S  P  N  D
B  D  C  C  E  P  C  S  D  U  T  N  X
```

BEDTIME	FRUITS	SLEEP
BREAKFAST	HEALTHY	SPORTS
DINNER	LUNCH	SWIM
EXERCISE	PLAY	VEGETABLES
FOOD	RUN	WALK

Get to Know God

Have you ever thought about God? I mean, He is a pretty big subject. You can't see Him or talk to Him on the phone, and some people don't even believe He exists.

But the Bible says, "Wisdom [or being smart!] begins with respect for the Lord" (Prov. 9:10).

So, if you want to be really smart, you'll get to know God.

How do you do that? How do you even know for sure that God exists?

Well, one way is to look around at this great, big, beautiful world we live in. Doesn't it make sense that somebody created all this—you know, the sun, the moon, the Pacific Ocean, Vermont, Lake Erie, and the Grand Canyon—instead of it just sort of happening by accident? It actually takes more faith to believe all this happened by chance than to believe somebody put it all together for a purpose.

Think of it this way. You wouldn't believe it if somebody just threw all the pieces of a watch into a paper bag, shook it up, and—presto!—out came a perfectly designed watch. Not very likely. Just like our world, a watch needs a designer—a smart one. When you think about mountains, oceans, trees, oxygen, and animals, you've got to start thinking that somebody made all this stuff.

Think about our eyes. Or the way we can grab stuff with our hands. Or think about our brains. No computer in the whole world can think as fast or as well as our brains. Seems pretty likely that someone pretty big and smart created all this stuff.

So, if God really does exist, how do you get to know Him? We'll talk about a few ways throughout this book.

Here's one way to start with: Begin by reading His story in the Bible. Bibles are easy to find. You might even have a Bible app on your phone or computer. Read Genesis in the Old Testament, the very first book of the Bible. It tells how God created everything and then goes on to tell the stories of a bunch of His people—Noah, Abraham, Jacob, Joseph, and lots of others. Then check out the New Testament. That's where you'll read the account of how God became a man—you heard that right—and how He came to earth to let us know what God was like.

By the way, that man's name was Jesus. We'll talk more about Him later.

13 Spend Time with God

If you have a best friend, what do you do to get to know them? Spend time with them, of course! But how do you spend time with, you know, God? After all, didn't He create everything in the entire universe?!?! You can't just invite Him over for dinner or send Him an email!

Even though you can't invite God to dinner or get Him on the phone, there are still ways to get to know Him. As we learned in the last chapter, the best way to get to know God is by reading the Bible. After all, it's His letter to us. God gave us His Word—the Bible—so we could get to know Him. So, here's a cool plan to get to know God a little bit more every day.

Try to spend a few minutes each day with God. It might be ten minutes in the morning right when you get up or sometime in the evening before bed. Whatever time works best for you, try this little routine:

1. Read your Bible for five minutes (or longer). Before you start reading, ask God to show you something about Himself as you read. You could start in the first book of the Bible, Genesis. Or you might start in the first book of the New Testament, Matthew. It tells a bunch of cool stories about Jesus, and it was written by a guy named Matthew, a tax collector who was an eyewitness to Jesus's life—somebody who was right there when it all happened.

2. After you read a little bit, try writing what you learned from the Scripture passage in a journal. Did you see something you didn't know about God, yourself, or other people while reading? Write it down!

3. Take a couple minutes to pray to God. We'll talk a little bit more about prayer later but know that prayer is just talking to God. Let Him know how you're doing, and thank Him for all the good things He's done for you. Take some time to ask Him to help other people you know. And then ask Him to help you with whatever's going on with you.

We'll talk a little more about the Bible in the next chapter.

God loves it when we spend time with Him. Here are some questions to help you do that.

1. According to this chapter, what are some ways we can spend time with God?

2. Have you ever read some of the Bible? Was it confusing to you? It might be a good idea to find a Bible that's designed for kids your age. That should help you understand it even better.

3. If you've read the Bible before, what were your favorite stories? Share about them and why you liked them.

When you're all done answering the questions, pray for one another. Share some things you'd like to ask God to help you with.

 **Get to Know the Bible**

Did you know that the Bible is God's love letter to us? It tells us all about God, how much He loves us, and even some of the cool things He's done on earth. The Bible is divided into two parts. The Old Testament talks about God's people, the Jews, from the beginning of time up through Noah's ark, the kings, and the prophets. There's also poetry, such as the Psalms and Proverbs. The New Testament talks about Jesus and His followers.

When you first start reading your Bible, it might seem kind of confusing, especially if you have an older version that uses old-fashioned language. But getting to know God and Jesus through reading your Bible is one of the most important things you can do. And it's easier than you think!

Here are a few things you can do right now to get to know your Bible:

1. Find a Bible that's aimed at your age group. Nowadays there are all kinds of Bibles for kids including ones that have pictures, maps, and even little study guides to help you know what's going on. Some even have devotional pages that help you apply what the Bible says to your everyday life.

2. Even though the Bible starts on page 1 like most books, it's probably best to start your reading in the

New Testament. The four Gospels—Matthew, Mark, Luke, and John—all tell the things that Jesus did while He was here on earth. There are cool stories about how Jesus healed people, taught people, and even raised a few from the dead!

3. It's a good idea to read your Bible every day either in the morning when you first get up or right before you go to bed. Just decide to read for maybe five to ten minutes a day. Anyone can do that much. Ask God to show you something in His Word when you read it and He will!

If you don't have a Bible, not to worry! You can find an inexpensive kids Bible online or at a bookstore. Your church might have one you can have, or there are Bible apps for your computer or phone. Either way, before you know it, you'll be learning God's Word and getting to know Him better and better!

Learn How to Cook Something

Learning how to cook something is really fun and a great way to feel more grown up. Don't worry, you don't have to bake up a ten-course meal with side dishes and dessert right off, but learning how to cook some simple meals will give you a great feeling of accomplishment. Plus, it'll be fun, and you get to eat it once you're done!

Important Tip! Keep this in mind when you decide to cook something. Make sure an adult is right there with you as you work with the stove, with the oven, or with knives. They'll keep things safe, help you with ingredients, and give you useful tips along your way to culinary greatness! (That just means you'll be a chef before you know it.)

Following are some suggested meal ideas and simple recipes you might try:

Microwave Mug Cake

This is a really easy, delicious, and quick dessert or afternoon snack. Gather all your ingredients, follow the directions, microwave, and enjoy!

Ingredients:

¼ cup all-purpose flour

¼ cup white sugar

2 tablespoons unsweetened cocoa powder

⅛ teaspoon baking soda

⅛ teaspoon salt

3 tablespoons milk

2 tablespoons olive oil

1 tablespoon water

¼ teaspoon vanilla extract

Directions:

1. Mix the flour, sugar, and cocoa powder in a mixing bowl. Add the baking soda, salt, milk, oil, water, and vanilla, then stir until you've got a liquid.
2. Pour the mixture into a big microwave safe mug.
3. Microwave for forty-five seconds. Remove from the microwave and let cool for a minute, then dig in!

   PS: For extra gooeyness, throw in some semi-sweet chocolate chips.

Microwave Mini Pizzas

These are great for a snack or even for a family dinner. Top your pizza with all of your favorite toppings.

Ingredients:

English muffins
Pizza sauce
Shredded mozzarella cheese
Precooked salami or pepperoni

Added toppings:
Pineapple pieces
Tomato slices
Red peppers, chopped
Carrot slices

Directions:

1. Slice the English muffins in half and place on a microwave-safe plate (for extra crunchiness, toast the muffin halves in the toaster for a couple of minutes first).
2. Spread some pizza sauce over the top of each muffin half.
3. Top the sauce with the shredded cheese and precooked salami or pepperoni.
4. Add other toppings like pineapple, tomatoes, red peppers . . . whatever you want! (Maybe not chocolate chips!)
5. Place the plate in the microwave, and cook for about two minutes.
6. Remove the plate and let the pizzas cool for a couple of minutes, then enjoy!

ⅢⅢⅢⅢⅢⅢ Chocolate Banana Smoothie ⅢⅢⅢⅢⅢⅢ

This is a yummy, quick, good-for-you shake you can enjoy anytime!

Ingredients:

1 to 2 handfuls of ice
1½ cups milk (you can also use vanilla almond or soy milk)
¼ cup vanilla yogurt, nonfat or low fat
2 large bananas
1 tablespoon chocolate hazelnut spread, such as Nutella

Directions:

1. Put the ice, milk, and yogurt into a blender.
2. Add the bananas (you might slice them or break them up for easier blending) and the chocolate hazelnut spread to the blender.
3. Place the lid tightly on the blender, and blend for twenty seconds.
4. Pour into your favorite glass and enjoy!

⦙⦙⦙⦙ **Peach Strawberry Yogurt Popsicles** ⦙⦙⦙⦙

This is a fun, delicious, and healthy way to enjoy a sweet treat for dessert or a snack on a warm afternoon. You might need an adult to help you with measuring and blending.

Ingredients:

3 cups strawberries, pureed in a blender to 1½ cups
3 cups peaches, peeled and sliced, pureed in a blender to make 1½ cups
2 tablespoons of honey
½ cup Greek vanilla yogurt

Directions:

1. In a blender, puree strawberries with 4 teaspoons of honey. Put the mixture in a bowl. Clean the blender.
2. Add the sliced peaches to the blender with 2 teaspoons of honey and puree. Put into a separate bowl.
3. In a popsicle mold (or in small paper cups if you don't have a mold), layer the popsicles as follows: 2 teaspoons strawberry puree, 1 teaspoon yogurt, and 2 teaspoons peach puree. Repeat layers until the mold is full.
4. Tap the mold on the counter to make sure all of the layers settle. If you want, you can use a spoon to swirl the mixture.
5. Insert the popsicle sticks and then freeze for at least six hours or overnight.

Easy Scrambled Eggs

This recipe makes a great quick breakfast, but why not try eggs for dinner occasionally?

Ingredients:

¼ teaspoon butter

4 eggs

Pinch of salt and pepper

2 slices of whole-grain toast

1 tablespoon cold water

Directions:

1. Melt the butter in a small frying pan on the stove. This will help the eggs to not stick to the pan. Have an adult help you with this!
2. Crack the eggs into a bowl, add water, and whisk with a fork until well blended.
3. Add the salt and pepper to the eggs.
4. Pour the eggs into the hot pan.
5. Stir regularly until the eggs are cooked through. Make sure they're not runny.
6. Remove from pan, and put onto a plate. Serve them with the toast and jam.

16 Discover and Be Who God Wants You to Be

One of the best ways to have a great life is to figure out who God made you to be. Did you know that God has known you since before you were born? Whoa, that's a weird thought, isn't it? And not only does He know you, but He also has big plans for you!

"What do you mean big plans? I'm only a kid!" you might say.

But think about the dreams you have for your life. What are some of the things you love to do? Draw, play soccer, explore, do science experiments, play with your cat? Do you like to make your friends and family laugh? Are you really good at solving puzzles?

Most of the time, God uses the things we already love (and are good at) to make our lives richer and more fun but also to make us a blessing to others.

What are some of the things God has put inside of you that He might use to make you a blessing?

If you like science and helping people, He might make you a doctor.

If you like writing stories, He might lead you to use your gifts to become an author.

If you love sports, you might become a sports star or a high school coach.

If you love music or singing, that might be part of God's plans for you.

If you like fixing things, He might make you an engineer or a designer.

If you love animals, you might become a veterinarian or work on a farm.

Get the point? As we discover the things God's put inside each one of us, we can do our part—study, practice, learn, and get help. And as we grow, we can watch and partner with the Lord to become all—and even more—than we could ever dream!

TALK IT OVER

Isn't it exciting that God not only knows who you are but also has big plans for your future?

1. Why do you think God has plans for you?

2. Name some of the things you love to do. What are some things you're really good at? Sometimes these might be the same things.

3. After you've named some of the things you're good at, discuss ways that God might use these gifts He's given you to be a blessing to other people. For example, if you're really good at spelling, you might help another kid with his spelling list.

17 Handling Homesickness

It's always fun to experience a new adventure with family and friends. An adventure like a sleepover or even a trip to an overnight camp can be really fun and exciting, and it's a chance to feel grown up. But sometimes, once you get to the new place—whether it's a friend's house or a summer camp—you might start to feel a little . . . homesick.

You know, that feeling of nervousness because you're in an unfamiliar place and you miss your mom, your dad, maybe even your cat, and your own bed. But at the same time, you don't want to miss out on the fun, so what do you do? Well, the first thing to remember is you're not alone in feeling this way! Lots of kids feel a little nervous about being away from home, especially if it's the first time. Think about it. They even have a name for it—*homesickness*. So it makes sense that lots of other people feel the same way too!

Here are a few ideas to help you when you're feeling a little homesick:

1. **Share your feelings.** First of all, talk to your parents or a trusted adult about your feelings. Even if you're not at camp or your friend's house yet, let them know ahead of time that you're a little concerned that you'll miss home a lot. Come up with some ideas of how you can manage those feelings and how you can respond if you feel homesick while you're there. And you can tell

God how you're feeling. Do you ever wonder if Jesus got homesick for heaven while He was here on earth?

2. **Ask questions.** If you're going away to camp, find out how bedtime works: What if you have to go to the bathroom during the night? What are some ways you can calm yourself if you can't go to sleep? Call the camp and ask how they handle homesickness.

3. **Spy out the land.** If you can, visit the place you'll be staying ahead of time so you can get an idea of how things work. If it's camp and it's too far away, check out their website or Facebook page. Look at photos of the layout of the camp and watch videos of the activities. Try to take the mystery out of the experience even before you get there.

4. **Try a dry run!** Have a sleepover with a kid who lives on your street or close by. Or maybe just stay at their house till bedtime. Try sleeping in your sleeping bag at home for a few nights. If the camp you want to visit has day camps, try one of those. Once you get used to a day camp, the next step is often a sleepover.

5. **Take some home with you.** Bring a familiar item from home with you to the camp or sleepover. Your favorite stuffed animal or even your pillow from home might make you feel more comfortable. Take along a photo of your family or pets. Any one of these things will help make your camp home feel more like your family home.

DID YOU KNOW?

The national animal of Scotland is a unicorn. Scots believe the unicorn represents purity, innocence, and power.

 # Don't Be Afraid

What kinds of things scare you? Scary movies? Noises outside late at night? Monsters? Being alone? The DARK?!?!

Did you know that almost everyone in the world is scared of something? Spiders, dogs, heights, and maybe clowns! Yes, even adults—teachers, scientists, pastors, and celebrities—have things they're afraid of.

Do you worry about something that might happen in the future? Something at school, at home, or in your neighborhood? Are you afraid something might happen to a friend or family member? That's a really normal thing, so you don't ever have to feel ashamed if you have some fears in your life.

Now, of course, in some cases it's smart to be fearful. It's good to be cautious when you're crossing the street or swimming in a lake. You don't want to approach a strange dog unless you ask the owner if it's all right, and you don't want to go rock climbing without the proper gear and an adult to help you.

But if you find yourself getting fearful about things and it's making you feel stuck, here's a great thing to remember—God is always with you! He promises never to leave you alone or forget about you.

When we worry, it's like we're imagining something in the future where God won't be there to help us. But just like God is with you *right now*, He will also be there when you need Him *in the future*! God is always *with* you and always *for* you. Here are a couple verses from the Bible to remind you that you don't ever have to be afraid:

So don't be afraid. The Lord your God will be with you everywhere you go. (Josh. 1:9)

When I am afraid, I will trust you [God]. (Ps. 56:3)

So, no matter what you might be afraid of, remember that God knows all about it, and He'll help you through whatever it is. Just ask Him to help you and He will!

Learn How to Handle a Bully

Unfortunately, almost every kid has to deal with a bully sometime in their life. It's no fun. You feel helpless and like you can't stand up for yourself. But not to worry. There are some simple things you can do to handle this awkward and scary situation.

First of all, it's important to remember that being bullied is never your fault. Almost always, kids who bully don't feel very good about themselves, and rather than deal with their own problems, they pick on other kids. Here are some tips you might try if you come upon a bully:

1. Walk confidently, standing up straight and with your head held up. Don't look down at the ground when you walk around. Bullies usually pick on the kids who look insecure.

2. Confidently use phrases with the bully like "Leave me alone," "That wasn't nice," or "Yeah, whatever," then walk away. Use the bully's name and stand back. Keep your voice calm. Doing this right off usually keeps things from escalating and getting worse.

3. If you feel comfortable enough, try using humor. "Yeah, you're right. I am pretty skinny. When I turn sideways, I disappear. I have to run around in the shower just to get wet." Sometimes humor calms the situation down.

4. If a bully is bothering you at school or in your neighborhood, do what you can to avoid them. If they always seem to find you on your way to music class or recess, go a different way. Change up the way you walk to school or where you sit on the bus. If they can't find you, they can't bully you.

5. Stick around your friends. Bullies rarely bother a kid who's in the middle of a group of friends. Make sure you've got someone with you at recess, lunchtime, and after school.

6. If someone's bullying you online, tell your parents right away, and even though it's tempting, don't respond to the bullying message. You might even want to unplug and stay off the computer for a while. You don't need to listen to that.

Don't ever feel bad telling an adult about a bully. You're not tattling. You need to let a teacher, a parent, or an aide know what's going on. Nobody should ever feel unsafe at school, at home, or anywhere else. You deserve better.

And let God know about what's happening. Pray for your safety and peace at school and elsewhere, and if you can, pray for the bully. Pray that they'll stop bullying people.

What are some other ways you can deal with a bully?

Keep Your Cool

Have you ever had one of those days when you really wanted to blow up? Somebody does something or says something, and you get so mad you want to yell and scream. Or hit the person. Or say something that really hurts *them*. We've all had those times. It's not like we plan to do something hurtful, but it all happens so fast. It just all comes out and we can't help it. It's like our happy brain turns off and our upset brain takes over.

So how do we get our happy brain back? Here are a few things you can do to calm your brain down and keep your cool. When you feel yourself getting ready to blow (you know the feeling— you might get all hot inside, your heart starts racing, you might even start to sweat), the first thing you should do is try to leave the situation. Even if you just take a few steps back. Or go into another room if you can. Give yourself a time-out.

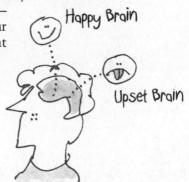

Then try these things to calm yourself and keep you out of trouble:

1. *Slow breathe.* Breathe in slowly to a
   count of four. Hold it for four, then slowly breathe out

to a count of eight. This slow breathing will slow your heart rate down and bring your happy brain back online. You may have to do this three or four times.

2. *Get physical.* There are a couple physical things you can do to calm down too. Try rubbing the bone behind your ear for a few seconds. This might help you calm down. Or cross your arms so that your hands are on your upper arms. Tap your left arm with your right hand four times. Then tap your right upper arm with your left hand four times. Do this five times.

3. *Tighten/release.* Tighten everything in your body from your toes all the way up to the top of your head. Even your face! Fingers, arms, legs, everything. Hold everything real tight for five seconds. Then do just the opposite. Let everything go loose like you're made of cooked spaghetti. This tighten/release exercise should help you calm down and feel more relaxed.

Hopefully, these simple exercises will help you keep calm and keep your cool when you feel like you're ready to blow.

Sometimes it's hard to calm down after someone does or says something that hurts you. But it's good for you and the people around you to learn how to calm yourself down.

1. Can you remember a time when you blew your top and said or did something that made things worse? What happened?

2. Out of the suggestions for calming yourself down (slow breathe, get physical, or tighten/release), which one do you think would work best for you when you get upset, anxious, or angry?

3. What kinds of things seem to upset you as you deal with other people? Share a few. How can you learn to avoid these things?

Use Good Manners

When you think of good manners, what comes to your mind? Sitting at a fancy table, trying to figure out which fork to use and how to eat your soup without slurping?

Well, those might be part of it, but having good manners is a lot simpler than that. In fact, chances are you're already using good manners most of the time anyway.

But here are a few tips on how to be polite and look pretty grown up when you're around other people—especially adults:

1. *Make eye contact.* This simply means when you meet someone or when you're talking to them, make sure you look them in the eye. Study what color their eyes are. Are they blue? Brown? Green? If you're looking away or looking down at the ground, it seems like you're insecure, and we all know you're not. So go ahead and smile and look them in the eye. You'll look and feel more confident.

2. *Let others go first.* If there's a line for food, or to go through a door somewhere or even to get into your classroom, don't try to push ahead and crowd everybody out. Let them go first.

3. *Hold the door.* When you're going through a door, look around to make sure nobody's behind you. If someone

is, open the door and hold it for them. That's just a cool thing to do.

4. *Use the magic words.* You probably learned this as a little kid but always say please when you're asking for something and thank you when you receive it. *Please, may I have a popsicle? Thank you for letting me pet your puppy.* Like that.

5. *Don't make a bad comment about someone's appearance.* Sometimes little kids blurt out things that aren't so nice. Like if someone is thin or heavy, they might say something about it. This can be really embarrassing for the other person. So even if you notice something about a person—a scar, their weight, an injury, or a disability—just keep it to yourself.

6. *Don't interrupt.* When you're talking to someone, wait until they finish talking before you say something. When they finish, then go ahead and speak.

See? Having good manners means thinking about the other person. It's not so hard, is it?

What are some other ways you can think of to show good manners?

Keep Your Room Clean

"You need to clean your room! It's a pigsty!" Ugh, who likes to hear those words? But the fact is keeping your room clean is a great way to keep your life calm and organized. Believe it or not, some people get anxious or upset when they're in a messy space.

Keeping your room clean isn't as hard as you think. Here are a few tips to help you keep your room clean and organized:

1. Sort your clothes as soon as you take them off. Hang up the ones you're going to wear again, and toss the dirty ones into the laundry basket.

2. It's probably not a good idea to eat in your room, but if you do have a snack or a drink in there, make sure you take the empty glass and plate back to the kitchen right away. After a few days, these things really begin to stink.

3. Keep your school stuff organized. If you have a desk, put your books, notebook, and papers in order on top. Clean out your backpack at least once a week, and throw away or recycle the old papers you don't need anymore.

4. Sometimes your bed or desk might get a little crowded during the week. So, on the weekend, go through your stuff and organize everything. If you do this every week, it'll be a lot easier to keep track of important things.

5. Learn how to make your bed so it looks nice. You might have your mom or dad show you the best way to do it. Then take over and make it yourself. It's a great thing to do every morning.

6. The BIGGEST cleaning tip of all is to take care of your room *every day*. If you hang up your clothes, make your bed, and keep your school stuff organized, you won't need to spend a long time on Saturday cleaning it up. You can spend that time playing, reading, or hanging out with friends!

Bonus Tip: Why not make collecting your dirty clothes into a competitive sport? Place a small basketball hoop on the wall above your laundry basket. Then toss your dirty clothes through the basket. That way you can practice shooting three-pointers with your T-shirts, shorts, and tops.

23 Watch Your Mouth! Part 1

Do you have trouble controlling what you say sometimes? Have you ever said anything that ended up hurting another person's feelings? Be honest, we all have. Proverbs 18:21 in the Bible says that we have the power of life and death in how we speak. That means we can either speak life into a situation or speak death—you know, something that isn't helpful or can even be hurtful. You might remember a time when someone called you stupid or ugly or said that nobody liked you. How did that feel? Pretty lousy, right? Well, learning how to control your speech is one of the best ways to grow up and be a good friend.

"But how do you do that?" you might ask. "Sometimes things just come out of my mouth!" Right? Well, here are a few things to think about before you say something that might hurt someone. Ask yourself the following:

1. *Is it true?* Make sure what you're saying is the truth. You sure don't want to be known as a liar whom people can't trust. Make sure you're always telling the truth.

2. *Is it needed?* Sometimes we end up saying things that really aren't important. Are you about to say something bad about a friend, a sibling, or even a teacher? Think about it. If it's not going to help anybody, you should probably stay silent.

3. *Does it build somebody up or tear somebody down?* Nowadays, it seems pretty cool to put people down with how we talk. You see it on TV and online all the time. But in real life, people tend to want to hang around people who make them feel better about themselves, not worse. If you had a friend who was always telling you what a loser you were, would you hang out with them very much? Probably not. Speak words that build people *up!*

If you have trouble controlling your tongue, ask God to help you. He wants you to be a blessing to people around you, and He'll help you out when it comes to how you speak. Just ask Him. You could pray something like this:

Dear Lord, help me to always speak the truth and to only say things that are important. Help me especially to build people up and not tear them down. Help me to talk to and about people the way I'd like them to talk to or about me.

 **Watch Your Mouth! Part 2**

In the last chapter, we talked about how we speak—saying things that are true, that are needed, and that build people up rather than tear them down. What about swearing and bad language? As you get older and into middle and high school, you may start to hear a lot more swearing at school. Your friends might even start to use bad language.

So, what do you do if the people around you are swearing all the time?

This is a hard one, mainly because almost everywhere you go you might hear bad language. TV, movies, even some video games include it, so it's easy to get in the habit of using it too. The best way to avoid using bad language is to never start.

Sometimes it seems really cool or even grown-up to use swear words when you're talking, but it actually shows a lack of imagination and can even make you sound silly. And you want to sound smart, don't you?

So how do you avoid getting in the habit of using bad words even if the people around you are using them?

First, ask God to put a guard on your mouth right now—today—and He will.

Then, when you feel like using bad language, stop for a second. Take a deep breath and give your mind (and your mouth!) a chance to decide if you really want to use it. The more you think about how you want to speak, the easier it will be to limit the bad words that might come out of your mouth.

If you've already found yourself starting to use bad language, ask God to help you think before you speak, and He will. He wants you to watch your mouth!

Have you ever noticed that your mouth is the hardest thing in your body to control? God wants to help you speak words of life to the people around you.

1. Have you ever said anything hurtful to someone without thinking? What happened?

2. Is it true? Is it needed? Does it build someone up? Which one of these is the hardest for you to check before you speak?

3. Is it hard for you not to use bad language occasionally? According to this section, what are some ways to stop doing that?

Start a Friendship with Jesus

We talked about getting to know God a little while ago, but what does it mean to start a friendship with Jesus? First of all, it's probably good to know who Jesus is—He's God in human form! About two thousand years ago, God became a man—in fact, that's what Christmas is all about. God was born as a baby just like all of us! Jesus grew up, and when He became an adult, people started to realize that He was pretty special. He healed people from sickness, He did some amazing miracles like calming a storm and walking on water, and He taught people about how much God loved them.

But Jesus's main purpose for coming to earth was to bring us back to God the Father.

Because God is perfect and we're not—we do bad stuff—we're separated from God. So, He came up with a great plan. He sent Jesus to come and live a perfect life and then to take on Himself the punishment for all the bad stuff we do. He became a sacrifice for us; He took our place. Jesus was hung on a cross where He died. But even more important, He was separated from God His Father so that we never have to be!

The good news is that after He died, Jesus rose from the dead three days later! And He's alive now and with God the Father forever. This may sound pretty crazy, but it's all true! And because of Jesus's sacrifice, we never have to be separated from God ever again. In fact, we can live forever with Him in heaven!

Even though we all do bad stuff, we can be forgiven and begin a friendship with Jesus. It's pretty simple.

We can follow the ABCs of starting a friendship with Jesus:

Admit that you do bad stuff and that there's no way you can ever be good enough to go to heaven.

Believe that Jesus is who He said He is—God's Son—and that He lived a perfect life and then went to the cross, died, and was separated from the Father so we never have to be. Also, believe that Jesus beat death by rising from the dead to live forever.

Confess that Jesus isn't just your best friend but the King, the Ruler, the Boss of your life, and choose to follow Him wherever He leads you. He's got big plans for you!

God's Treasure

Did you know you're God's treasure? Follow the maze and help these kids dive down and find the sunken treasure chest.

Shop for Groceries

Want to feel grown up? There's nothing like a trip to the grocery store to help you feel independent and like an adult (other than driving maybe, but you'll probably have to wait a few years for that). Now, of course, unless you live next door to a market, you'll probably need a parent to go with you, but you can still do a lot of the shopping yourself. Here are a few tips for grocery shopping:

1. If you have more than two or three items to pick up, you should first make a list. Write down if you need to get milk, bread, cereal, toothpaste, and so on. That will help you stay organized once you get to the store.

2. After a few visits, you'll probably start to learn where things are located in your local market. Check out the following sample store map to help you get the idea. Usually, milk, cheese, and yogurt—you know, dairy foods—are in the refrigerator section near the back of the store. Bread and rolls are in the bakery, and fresh

fruits and vegetables usually have their own sections over on one side of the store.

3. If you're paying for your groceries with cash, see if you can figure out how much change you should be getting back. If your mom or dad gave you $20.00 and your groceries came to $17.25, how much change should you be getting back? (That's right, $2.75.)

4. After a while, you might want to start figuring out how you can save money on certain items. Sometimes buying a larger size of a product can end up being cheaper than the smaller size. Or if certain items are on sale that week, it might be a good idea to stock up.

And your mom or dad might have a coupon on their phone or cut out from the newspaper that can save you money on groceries too.

Sample Grocery Store Map

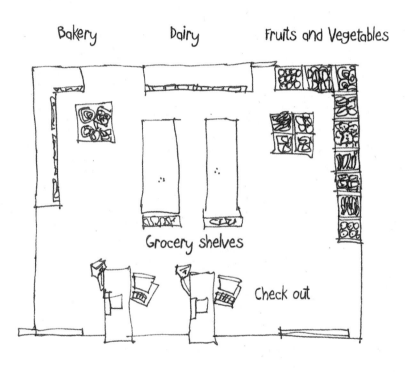

Bakery   Dairy   Fruits and Vegetables

Grocery shelves

Check out

Entrances

27 Do Your Own Laundry

If you're older than seven or eight, you should be able to do your own laundry in the washing machine. It's really easy, but make sure you have your mom or dad show you how to do it the first few times. Here are some simple tips to help you:

1. First, gather all your dirty clothes. You know, stuff you've worn once or twice already during the week. Don't forget anything—shorts, shirts, underwear, socks—you get the idea. A great way to keep them all together is to have a box or basket in your room where you toss your dirty clothes.

2. You might want to separate all the colored clothes, like red T-shirts, blue jeans, and colored shorts, from the white things, like white socks, T-shirts, and underwear. Put whichever clothes you're going to do first in the washing machine. Don't overload it.

3. Now here's the only tricky part of this whole process— how much detergent to put in. Your mom or dad can show you how much to add. If you don't put in enough, your clothes won't get clean, and if you put in too much, they might come out kind of slimy.

4. Next, set the knob for hot, cold, or warm water (usually you'll use warm), then push the button, and that's it! Easy, huh?

5. The wash usually takes between thirty and forty-five minutes. It might buzz or ding or something to let you know it's done, but you can tell because the machine will stop and be quiet. Wait a couple minutes to make sure it's finished.

6. Take the wet clothes out of the washing machine and load everything into the dryer. Your mom or dad can show you how to set the knob for the amount of time you need to dry the clothes.

7. After about thirty to forty minutes, the clothes should be dry and ready to take into your room and put away. Either hang them up or fold them and put them in your dresser. And there you have it! Clean clothes for the next week or so!

Look for the Good in People

Chances are you've got some good friends that you like to hang around with. You like to laugh together and play games together. You can just be yourself when you're around them. Then there are some people who, well, aren't that much fun to be around. They might be really negative or always telling you what you're doing wrong, or they might just be cranky all the time. So, what is the right thing to do?

You might think, *RUN AWAY! I don't want to be around those people!* And in some cases, you might be right. You don't have to hang around people who always make you feel lousy. BUT if you have no choice, maybe they're in your class or your church, here's a clue for how to respond: Try to find something *good* about them.

"WHAT?" you might say. "I can't think of one thing that's good about them. They drive me crazy!"

Well, think hard. There must be something that's good about them. Look carefully and think outside the box.

Maybe they've got cool shoes or a fun backpack.

Or they love their dog and take really good care of him.

Or they're really good at spelling.

Or maybe they're a talented artist or musician.

Or they have a nice sister.

You see? Try really hard to find something good about the person. Ask God to help you, and you might be surprised. He'll show you some good things about the person who might be driving you crazy. You might not end up being best friends with that person, but at least you'll be able to learn to get along with them. That'll make life easier for them—and you! Look for something good.

29 Learn What Kind of Learner You Are

Did you know that different kids learn in different ways? "Huh, what does this mean?" you might ask. "I learn stuff because I want to know about it, right?" Well, yes, but there are three main types of learning. When you see what they are, chances are you'll discover what kind of learner *you* are. It's important to know how you learn best because when you know that, you'll have a better time in school, and you'll remember what you learn a whole lot more! *So, what are the three types of learning?* I'm glad you asked.

1. *Seeing.* A lot of us learn best by *seeing* something. That's why a lot of teachers use photos, flashcards, posters, Power-Point, and videos when they're teaching. This is called visual learning, and most people remember a lot more when they *see* something than when they just hear it. Is this you? If it is, then you'll learn well by reading or watching something.

2. *Hearing.* Some people, not many, learn best just by hearing something. If someone *tells* them something, like where the Nile River is (it's in Egypt), they'll remember it. Sometimes it might take a few times of hearing the information, but

listening is the best way for these kids to remember. If this is you and you learn best by hearing something, a teacher standing up in front of the class and speaking is going to be your best bet for learning.

3. *Touching.* This is called tactile learning, and it just means that you learn best by doing something. You might *hear* about a scientific experiment, but it won't really mean much to you until you actually do it for yourself. Once you've experienced something, you'll usually remember it for a long time. If you're a tactile learner, it might be good for you to write down what the teacher is talking about or even draw a picture as you listen. These are helpful ways for a tactile learner to remember things.

Do any of these learning styles sound familiar to you? If you still can't figure out which way you learn best (you might be a combination of more than one), ask your mom or dad or teacher to help you figure out which one fits you. Once you learn your learning style, you'll really start to shine in your school or homeschool work.

 # Pray Joyfully!

You might pray to God all the time, or this might be the first time you've ever even thought about it. But praying is really cool, and it's one of the biggest privileges we have in this life. Think of it this way: What if you could speak to the president of the United States anytime you wanted? Or maybe you'd like to speak to your favorite sports or music star? You'd do it, wouldn't you?

By praying, you're actually speaking to the Creator of the entire universe! In fact, He created the president and all the sports and music stars you can think of.

"Sounds good," you might say, "but how do I do it? I don't know how to pray. Are there certain words I need to use? Don't I need to kneel or fold my hands or something?" No, not at all. When you pray, just think of God as your best friend. Let Him in on what's going on with you.

Are you feeling happy? Did you just join a team? Score a goal? Learn a new song on the piano? Let God know about it. Lots of times in the Bible God is referred to as our Father, and a father wants to know everything that's going on with his kids.

Are you feeling upset? Mad? Lonely? Jealous? Let Him know that, too, and ask for His help with the things you are feeling.

Don't worry about using all the right words or standing a certain way. Just talk to Him. It might seem funny at first because you can't see Him, but faith is trusting that God hears you, even when you can't see Him.

You might try praying something like this:

Dear Lord, I'm really thankful for your help with my test today. Thank you for my family and my dog [or cat!] and school too. But I need your help now with _____.
I know You love me, and I pray that You'll show me what to do. And help me be a good friend to people and to love them like You love me.

See how simple that is? Go ahead and try it.

PS: You can talk to God anytime you want. You don't have to wait for nighttime or morning or going to church to talk to Him. He's always there, and He's ready to listen.

Try to See Things from Other People's Point of View

Just like we mentioned in chapter 28, there are going to be some people in your life you just don't like. They might be mean or they tease you all the time or they're just no fun to be around. Can I tell you a secret on how to get along with a person like that? Try getting *curious*.

"What does that mean?" you ask.

It means starting to wonder what's going on with them. Sometimes kids (and adults) are going through hard things, and instead of letting you know about them, the stress from the hard things comes out in different ways. They might act mean or angry or even blame you for stuff you didn't do.

Here's an example: Let's say there's some kid on the playground who's being mean to everyone. He hogs the ball, he gets mad when he gets out, or he yells at all the other kids. Somebody like that is no fun to play with, are they?

But there might be more to his story. There could be things going on in his life that are making it hard for him.

What if his parents just got divorced? Or what if one of his parents is sick, or one of them has left the family and the kid is scared? What if the kid has never learned to read or write? So, instead of saying, "Hi, my name is Marcus and my parents just got divorced" or "I can't read," he just acts angry and mean all the time.

So, what do you do?

Get curious. Before you respond in a mean way, maybe count to ten. Pray for this kid. And if the time is right, you might even say, "Are you okay? It seems like something's going on and you can tell me." They may or may not tell you what's going on, but at least they'll know you care. Keep praying and keep getting curious; there's almost always a reason behind somebody's bad behavior. (For more tips about how to handle a bully, check out chapter 19.)

PS: If somebody is picking on you, threatening you, or bullying you in any way, they're not your friend. Stop hanging around them, and let an adult know what's happening.

Getting curious might be a new way of thinking for you. Sometimes, there are things going on in a kid's life you don't know about. Talk about how you might start getting curious with friends at school or in your neighborhood.

1. Why do you suppose kids (and adults!) don't always share the hard things they're going through?
2. What are some new ways you can react when somebody's being mean or angry?
3. Do you ever have bad days? How do you act when you're feeling this way?

Love and Care for Animals

When God created the world, He made all kinds of cool animals—blue whales, buffalos, tigers, elephants, and zebras. He created some unusual looking creatures like hippos and giraffes and some really funny ones like penguins and monkeys. He created some really cool birds like eagles and blue herons, and He made some tiny little creatures like ladybugs and ants.

Then He made people, and He gave the man, Adam, the job of naming the animals. Can you imagine how big a job that must have been? Later God gave Adam and his wife, Eve, the task of taking care of all the animals.

God loves it when we take care of the animals around us too. You might have a dog or a cat. You love your pets as if they were family, but they can't take care of themselves. They need food and fresh water every day, but they can't fix food for themselves or pour fresh water into their bowls. For the most part, they can't even open doors by themselves. Your dog might need a walk every day or your kitten might need some exercise, so you need to play with them. God made them this way. They depend on us, and we have the responsibility of taking care of them. And it's important to be kind to any animal you're taking care of. Never mistreat or neglect them. And give them plenty of love. They need you.

Taking care of animals goes beyond just the animals in our homes. We might have a chance to rescue a lost kitten or help a friend find their dog who ran away. Being kind to and taking good care of animals is a great way to live a good life.

What are some ways you can take care of the animals in your life? Even if you don't have a pet, can you think of ways you can still love animals?

33 Learn to Be Quiet and Listen

If you're like most kids, you love to share your ideas and thoughts about things. I mean, who has better ideas than you? But did you know that one of the most important life skills you can learn as a kid growing up is how to listen? "What? Listen? I do that all the time!" you might say. Sure, of course, people are always talking to you—parents, teachers, friends, neighbors, even the people on TV or online.

But have you learned to really *listen*?

Here's a little life hack if you really want to grow up and learn some important things: Learn how to listen! Believe it or not, the people around you might have some good things to tell you.

If you're learning how to play baseball or soccer, it's a good idea to listen to the coach, right? They've done this a few times and probably know what they're talking about.

If you want to learn how to make a grilled cheese sandwich or some chocolate chip cookies, have your mom or dad show you how to do it and listen while they're explaining it.

If you're trying to learn how to spell or do multiplication, listen to your teacher. Really listen, and ask questions if you need to.

And the first thing you need to do when you're listening is to be quiet. That's a hard one sometimes, isn't it? But if you're always interrupting (even with good questions), chances are you're not really listening.

Check this out. Is this you? Sometimes (and we all do this) when someone else is talking, you're not really listening; you're thinking about what you're going to say next. So instead, try to focus on what the other person is saying. It might take some practice, but you'll learn to be a great listener this way.

And you want to know a secret? A good way to make friends is to ask questions and then really listen to people as they answer. Remember the things they're saying. People want to be known, and listening is one of the best ways to do that.

And if you want to know if you have a really good friendship with someone, ask yourself, *Am I listening to them, and are they listening to me?* A good friendship goes both ways.

 # Learn Something New Every Day

One of the best ways to keep your brain sharp and active is to make sure you learn something new every day. Of course, you'll probably learn something every day in class—if you're listening—but there are lots of other things you can learn throughout the day.

You might learn what a friend's favorite sport or hobby is.

You might find out that someone you know owns a horse!

You could practice memorizing all the states that make up the United States starting with where you live.

You might learn how to draw a whale.

You might find out how many planets there are or if Pluto is still a planet.

As you go through your day, look around and see if there's something new you can learn.

Here's an idea: Get ahold of a journal or even a little notebook and write down what you learned that day. It might be something as simple as your substitute teacher's name or something more challenging like, What's the smallest country in the world?*

Write it down, and by the end of the year you'll have a journal full of all kinds of interesting stuff.

*Vatican City, in the middle of Rome where the pope, the head of the Catholic Church, lives.

Some families play, What did you learn today? at the dinner table every night. That's a good way to practice remembering the new stuff you're learning as well as getting to share it with your family.

Try to learn something new every day!

DID YOU KNOW?

In one of the original versions of the fairy tale Cinderella, her fairy godmother was a cat.

Learn to Make Good Decisions

We make lots of decisions every day, sometimes without even realizing it. What game to play? What show to watch? What T-shirt to wear? Should I go eat lunch with Olivia? But as you grow up, some of the decisions you're going to make will be really important. Who should I hang out with? What school should I go to? Should I try out for the baseball team?

So how do you learn to make good decisions—decisions that will really help you live a great life? Here are a few suggestions to help you make good choices:

1. *Find out what God thinks about it.* "Whoa. How do I know what God is thinking? He's, I mean, . . . GOD!" Here's one way: Check out His Word, the Bible. While the Bible won't tell you if you should try out for the team or what classes you should take, it does have some good advice about

   - Making friends: "Whoever spends time with wise people will become wise. But whoever makes friends with fools will suffer" (Prov. 13:20).
   - The work you do: "Everything you say and everything you do should all be done for Jesus your Lord. And in all you do, give thanks to God the Father through Jesus" (Col. 3:17).
   - And how to solve some of your problems: "Continue to ask, and God will give to you. Continue to search,

and you will find. Continue to knock, and the door will open for you" (Matt. 7:7).

So check out your Bible. It might help you make good decisions.

2. *Ask for advice.* Is there someone in your life you really trust? Maybe somebody a little older who might have some good advice for you as you make important decisions. Maybe your mom or dad, a teacher, or somebody from your church. Someone who loves God and who loves you. Find that person and let them know what's going on with you and the different choices you have to make. They'll help you figure out the best thing to do.

3. *Talk to God about it.* We talked about praying in chapter 30, and facing a hard decision is a great time to pray. When you have an important choice to make, take some time to ask God what you should do. You might say, "Dear God, I need Your help right now. Could You help me know what to do?" He might give you an idea you haven't thought of, He might bring somebody into your life to help you, or He might even open up circumstances to work out the thing you're trying to decide.

4. *Figure out what you'd like to do.* God created you with talents, skills, and desires, and they're there for a reason. If you have a strong desire to do something, and it's a good thing that God would approve of (see no. 1 in this list), chances are God wants you to do it. Sometimes He'll use our desires to lead us in the way to go.

5. *Watch how things work out.* This is one of those things you might not think about, but when you're trying to make a decision, watch how things work out. If you want to be an astronaut and you're only in the fourth grade, that may be one way God is saying, "Be patient, this may take awhile." But if you try out for the basketball team and they want you to be the captain, that's a good sign you're in the right place. Watch how things work out. That may be a way God is directing you.

36 Get Started

Sometimes the hardest thing about doing a job—especially one you don't like—is getting started.

Let's say your job is shoveling the snow off the sidewalk or picking up your dog's poop in the backyard. These are jobs nobody looks forward to. It's so easy to keep putting them off—"Oh, it's too cold" or "I'm too tired; I'll do it later."

But there are two problems with that:

1. The job won't ever get done.
2. The more you put it off, the bigger and harder the job seems to get. Have you ever noticed that?

So here are a couple ideas to get you started on whatever job you need to do:

Do just a little bit to start out. If you have a big homework assignment or a household chore to do, start off small. If you have twenty spelling words to learn, try learning just five of them. Anybody can do that, right? If you have to shovel the snow off the sidewalk, just shovel the steps and out to the mailbox. Then come back later and finish the front of the house. Breaking jobs into smaller tasks is a great way to help you get going. And remember, once you start, things get easier.

Set a time limit. Tell yourself, "Okay, I'm going to work on this math problem for ten minutes" or "I'm going to rake the leaves for fifteen minutes." That way the job doesn't seem so HUGE, and you'll feel good getting at it.

So, no matter what the job is, get going and get started!

PS: A funny thing happens when we set a time limit. Often, as we go ahead and start, we keep going and finish the job completely, which feels really good!

37 Pack Your Suitcase

When the suitcases come out, it usually means something fun is coming up. It might be a family vacation, a trip to summer camp, or even a weekend sleepover. But how do you pack, and what will you need? Here's a handy checklist to help make you a super-packer:

Clothes—Depending on how long you're going to be gone you'll need some pants or shorts, a few T-shirts, socks, and underwear. Is it going to be cool in the evening? Sometimes even summer nights can get chilly, so make sure to pack a sweatshirt or jacket. Don't forget shoes or sandals.

Personal stuff—This refers to things you might use in the bathroom. Remember your toothbrush and toothpaste, hairbrush, soap, and a washcloth (so you can wash your face before bed).

Comfort stuff—If you want, make sure you take your favorite stuffed animal or toy that reminds you of home. And maybe your favorite pillow.

If you're going on a big family vacation, especially if you're flying, your mom or dad can help you remember other things you'll want to take. You might want to pack a book or an activity to do while you're waiting for your flight.

And here's a tip: Don't just cram everything into your suitcase! Two reasons: One, all your stuff will get wrinkled and look bad, and two, if you fold and place the stuff inside, you'll be able to make room for everything and be able to find it once you get to the camp, island resort, sleepover, or whatever your final destination is.

When you and your suitcase are organized, you'll be set and ready to have a great time!

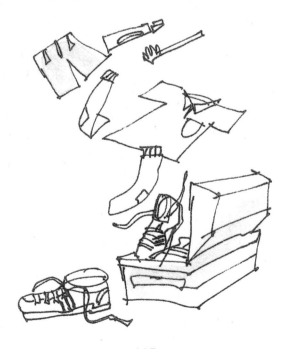

38 Learn How to Worship

You might ask, "How do we worship God? I mean, I sing songs with everybody else every time I go to church or my kids' class. Isn't that worship?"

Absolutely. Every time you sing songs to God in church, at a camp, or even at home, you're worshiping. And that's a good thing. But why is worshiping God so important?

For one thing, He's really worth it. Think about it. God created everything in the entire universe. He made the sun, the moon, and all the stars. He made the Mississippi River, the oceans, Colorado, and Argentina. And He made you! That's a good reason to worship God!

But another reason to worship Him is because He wants to be best friends with you. That's His number one priority—a friendship with you. That's pretty cool, wouldn't you say?

Plus, worshiping God reminds us how small we are and how GINORMOUS He is! And that helps us to know we can trust Him. There's no problem too big for God to handle. He's powerful, but He's also personal. He cares about every little and *big* thing going on in our lives.

So, how do we worship God? Do we only worship God when we're at church? No, not at all. And you don't even have to be a musician or singer to do it. Tell God thanks for helping you through your day at school or on the soccer field. That's worship! When you're about to go to sleep, tell Him how much you appreciate Him. Or when you wake up in the morning, you might say, "Good morning, Lord. So glad You're going to go through this day with me!" That's worship too.

Just knowing that God is good and that He loves you is a good way to start worshiping Him, whether you have music or not. Just tell Him how glad you are that He's your friend and that He wants you to get to know Him more and more every day. That's worship!

Learn How to Order in a Restaurant

Going out to eat is fun! I mean, who doesn't like to eat out? As you grow up, you might get the chance to start ordering from the menu yourself. Here are some things to think about when you get around to ordering your own meal.

If you're in a fast-food place, like McDonalds or Burger King, they'll have a giant menu up on the wall behind the workers. They'll usually have photos of the different kinds of burgers and sandwiches, and sometimes they'll even have a number by it. For example, a number 5 might be a single burger, fries,

and a drink. In that case you can just say, "I'll have a number 5, please." Always say please and thank you. These people work hard behind the counter, so it's good to be nice to them. Or you can say, "I'd like a single burger, fries, and a small drink, please."

If you go to a sit-down restaurant (yes, that's what they're called), then when you're seated, the host will hand you a menu. In a few minutes, a waiter or waitress will come to your table to take your order.

You might need a little help from your mom or dad at first, but the menu tells you what they're serving and how much everything costs. So, when you see something that looks good—like fish and chips or a grilled cheese sandwich with tomato soup—just tell the server, "I'd like the grilled cheese with tomato soup, please." See how easy that is?

Your parents can help you the first few times you do this, but pretty soon you'll be ordering off the menu like you do it all the time.

Accept Responsibility

My Bad!

You've made a mistake. We all do it, but you might be embarrassed or even ashamed. Nobody likes to admit they messed up. And the normal thing to do is to try to blame something or somebody else.

"He made me do it!"

"She started it!"

"The sun got in my eyes!"

"He should have done his part better!"

"They never told me!"

Sure, blaming somebody else might make you feel better at first, but you sure don't want to be known as the kid who never takes responsibility. When you make a mistake, it takes real courage to say, "My bad, that was my fault. Sorry."

Even though these are some of the hardest words to say, saying them will help you build healthy, lasting friendships and trust.

Plus, admitting you made a mistake and taking responsibility for it helps *you* in lots of ways:

1. You'll get to be known as someone who is trustworthy.

2. It gives you a chance to learn from your mistake.

3. Instead of spending all that energy coming up with excuses, you'll get a chance to figure out how to do it better next time.

So, the next time you goof up, remember, you can make things better by admitting your mistake. Just say, "My bad!"

Learn How to Fail

"What? Learn how to fail?" you might ask. "I thought failing meant you didn't do something well or really blew it. Anyone can do that without trying! Why do you need to *learn* how to fail?" Actually, what I mean is that you should learn how to *learn* something from failing. You're right, nobody wants to fail at anything they try—including learning how to throw a football, scoring high on a spelling test, jumping off the diving board, or riding a bike. Ouch, you especially don't want to fail at that.

But nobody does everything perfectly. Everybody fails sometimes. So, what should you do when your plans don't go according to . . . plan?

1. *Don't get bitter.* Nobody is perfect when they're trying something new. Try not to get discouraged or upset.

2. *Keep going!* Don't give up! Try it again! Sometimes when you don't succeed at something, you might want to quit. You know, stop trying. "What's the use? I'll never learn how to do this!" You might feel that way sometimes, but if you keep at it, chances are you're going to get a lot better at whatever it is you're trying to do. Keep going!

3. *Let God teach you through your failure.* Sometimes we learn our best lessons from the things we *don't* succeed

at. Ask God to show you what you did wrong and what to do next time to fix it.

4. *Remember, you're more than your failure.* Don't decide you're a failure just because you didn't succeed at one thing. It just happened. Think of all the other things you do really well!

5. *Realize when you fail what the good news is.* You tried something new. Not everybody does that. That's a whole lot better than not trying at all. The fact that you tried is awesome!

Thomas Edison, the inventor of the light bulb and the motion picture camera once said, "I have not failed. I've just found ten thousand ways that won't work."

Nobody likes to fail at something, but believe it or not, good things can come out of failing if you look hard enough.

1. Name a few things you're really good at. Sports? Music? School? Art? Helping?

2. Look at the list of what you're really good at. Can you remember when you first started any of them? Did it take awhile to learn? Did you maybe even fail at it a few times? How did that make you feel?

3. What are some things you can learn from failing at something? List a few.

Learn How to Handle Money

Do you get paid to do something? It might be doing your chores like walking the dog or taking out the trash, or maybe you have a job outside your home, mowing your neighbor's lawn or washing their car. However you make money, it's good to know how to manage it so you don't run out when you need it most, like right before Christmas or your cousin's birthday. Try the Save, Spend, and Give system to help you handle your money:

1. *Save*—When you get paid—let's say you make $10.00 for washing someone's car—it's a good idea to put some of that into savings. I know, it's really tempting when you've got money in your hand to want to SPEND it!!! "Wow, I think I'll buy a burger or some candy or the latest magazine." And that's cool. But if you want to have some money left for later for a bigger thing, like a bike, a new outfit, or a video game, you'll want to save some now. You might have a little bank in your room where you put the savings money, or you might even open up an account at a bank. A lot of people suggest saving 50 percent or half of the money that comes in. So, if you make $10.00, you might save $5.00.

2. *Spend*—You've got to spend *some* of that money, right? After all you're just a kid! So, if there's something you want right now, like a book, some food, or a treat, you

should feel free to buy it. Think about it, you've earned the money, you should be able to spend some of it! Maybe somewhere around 40 percent of the money or $4.00 out of your $10.00.

3. *Give*—This is the coolest part and something God wants us to do. There are a lot of people around who don't have enough money to get by. And in some places, there are even people who don't have anything to eat every day. Since God has given us so much, He wants us to share it with others. So, plan to give 10 percent or $1.00 of your $10.00 to help other people. You might give this to your church or Sunday school or an organization that helps the poor. We'll talk more about how to do this in the next chapter.

If you follow the Save, Spend, and Give system with your money, you'll be learning how to manage your money right now and in the future.

PS: God wants us to give 10 percent of what we make as a reminder that everything we have is a gift from him. Giving is a way of saying thank you to God.

Live Generously

As we learned in the last chapter, it's a good thing to give some of our money away to people who aren't as fortunate as we are. There are a lot of reasons why God loves it when we're generous. One is that it shows Him we realize that every good thing we have (including our money!) is a gift from Him. It's like we're saying, "Thanks, God, I realize that even my job or my allowance are from You." It's also a way to show that we're trusting Him to supply all our needs. Check out this promise:

> My God will use his wonderful riches in Christ Jesus to give you everything you need. (Phil. 4:19)

God also likes us to be generous because it helps other people. Did you know there are people in your state and maybe even your town who don't have enough to eat every day? So, whenever you give money to your church you might be helping someone nearby. Also, lots of cities have food banks that give away food for free to people who are struggling. You might think about giving them some food or a donation to help take care of these people.

And there are millions of people around the world who don't have enough food or even clean water to drink. There are some great organizations, like World Vision, Compassion International, and Samaritan's Purse, who are helping people get food and water. You can go online and see how you can support them. God says that every time you give money to help other people, you're giving to God!

> Then the King will answer, "I tell you the truth. Anything you did for any of my people here, you also did for me." (Matt. 25:40)

Living Generously

God loves it when we live generously. After all, all the good things we enjoy in life are gifts from Him. See how many of the words from the list below you can find.

```
S  E  S  N  V  V  I  J  P  G  N  N
I  C  B  S  P  D  M  Q  Q  I  L  Z  V
G  E  A  P  A  O  A  E  C  V  O  T  G
M  O  N  E  Y  L  I  W  N  I  L  S  S
G  O  K  N  C  L  G  R  C  N  S  C  E
A  S  R  D  S  A  V  I  N  G  T  L  M
E  M  F  I  S  R  S  C  J  M  R  J  E
O  C  E  N  T  S  S  H  A  R  E  E  L
E  L  I  G  E  N  E  R  O  U  S  C  J
N  O  D  M  Q  U  A  R  T  E  R  I  O
C  J  I  I  B  N  Q  I  L  N  R  M  L
N  D  N  I  C  K  E  L  G  V  L  N  O
J  L  E  E  E  O  Q  J  J  O  C  V  C
```

BANK	GENEROUS	RICH
CASH	GIVING	SAVING
CENTS	MONEY	SHARE
COINS	NICKEL	SPENDING
DIME	PAY	
DOLLARS	QUARTER	

Get Yourself Going

Are you a morning person? When you wake up are you full of energy and ready to face the day? Or do mornings make you want to roll over and go back to sleep, especially on school days? Well, the truth is no matter if you're a morning eager beaver or a "ten more minutes of sleep, please!" late riser, you'll need to get up and get yourself ready for school, even if you're homeschooled. So, what are some ways to make getting up and ready a little bit easier?

One thing you might do to help you out in the morning is to figure out the night before what you want to wear. Put out your jeans, shirt, and sweater so you'll have them ready to go when you get up. And get your shoes and socks ready too.

And once you're up, put your pj's away and make your bed.

Are you going to take a shower? Make sure you leave enough time for that. After a while, you'll see how much time you need to get ready in the morning. For some kids, it might be just fifteen minutes from bed to bus; for others, it might be a whole hour. Figure out which one you are and plan your morning according to how much time you're going to need.

Another good idea is to have your backpack, books, and papers that you'll need for school ready and by the door. That way you won't waste a bunch of time in the morning looking for last night's homework!

Will you be taking a lunch to school? If so, have all those ingredients close by. That way you can make a sandwich and grab an apple, chips, and a cookie or two and pack them in your lunch box quickly and easily. A lot of kids make their sandwich—or even pack their entire lunch—the night before.

And make sure you have something for breakfast too. It might be oatmeal, cold cereal, eggs, or toast with peanut butter and honey. Eating breakfast gives you energy and helps you focus as you go throughout the morning.

Getting a good start in the morning might just make your whole day go a lot better!

Let Someone Know When There's a Problem

Everyone has problems—kids, adults, grandmas and grandpas, pastors, teachers, and the guy who bags your groceries. So, you never need to be embarrassed or feel ashamed when things go wrong in your life. You might feel like a friend has rejected you because they went to play with somebody else and didn't include you. You might be having problems in school with certain subjects, or you might not feel like you're as good as the other kids on your team.

But you know what? Everyone has experienced those feelings! Everyone has felt left out and lonely or struggled in some way at school.

So, what do you do when something is going all wrong? One thing you should do for sure is let someone know about it! Sometimes you may feel embarrassed or ashamed because you feel like you're a failure. But that's not true. You need to have someone in your life you can talk to when you're going through a tough time. Somebody who loves you and will understand what you're going through. It might be your mom or dad or a teacher or someone from your church. It might even be an older brother or sister or your grandma.

God didn't create us to keep things that are bothering us inside. Keeping them inside just makes us anxious, sad, or feeling all alone. But sharing our hard stuff with someone else lifts the load off of us and allows another person to come alongside and share it. Plus, you might be surprised when you share. You might find out that the person you're sharing with has gone through the same thing you're going through! And together you might even come up with a solution to the problem you're facing.

So don't keep things you're struggling with inside; that's not good. Instead, find a person who loves God and who loves you and let them know what's going on. They'll be glad, and you will too.

PS: Did you know that Jesus understands everything you're going though? He knows what it's like to be anxious, rejected, disliked, and left out. And you can always tell Him what's going on no matter what it is and no matter where you are. He will always listen.

TALK IT OVER

Sometimes it's hard to ask for help when you're feeling sad, left out, or angry. Hopefully you're learning to tell someone when you have a problem.

1. It's fun to tell people about the good things going on in your life. Why is it harder to share your problems with them?

2. Do you remember a time when you shared a problem with your mom or dad or a friend? What happened? Did it feel good to share with them?

3. You know what happens sometimes when you let someone know you have a problem? Your friendship grows deeper, and then they feel like they can share with you too! If you're having a problem today, think of someone you know and trust that you can share it with.

 # Learn to Forgive

Have you ever been hurt by something someone has said or done? Of course, we all get hurt sometimes. It might have been by a classmate or a teammate, or even worse, you might have been hurt by a friend or your brother or sister.

It doesn't feel too good, does it?

So, what do you do about it? A typical thing to do or at least to *feel* like doing is to GET BACK AT THEM!!! Right? You'd like them to hurt as much as they hurt you. And that's pretty normal; after all, we're just human, aren't we? But that's not the best thing to do. The right thing to do is forgive them.

"Why?" you might ask. "They sure don't deserve it!" But there are a couple reasons we need to forgive people who have hurt us:

1. We ought to forgive because it helps us keep our friendship with someone else. Everybody makes mistakes. If they were mean to you or hurt you in some way, it might just be that they were having a bad day. You sure don't want to lose a friendship over a silly thing somebody said or did.

2. We ought to forgive because of what *not* forgiving does to *us*. When we don't forgive someone, it's like we want them to hurt just like they hurt us. But guess who gets hurt *more* when we don't forgive? That's

right, us! We end up continuing to be angry, upset, and even anxious when we don't forgive someone who's hurt us.

"What?!?! Forgive them after what they did to me?" Yeah, it's hard. But there are some steps to learning how to forgive someone who's hurt you.

First of all, forgiving them isn't going to be easy, and it might not happen right away. It's like when you hit your toe on a brick or the coffee table. It hurts for a while before you can even start to think straight. The same is true when our feelings get hurt. It might take an hour, a day, or even several days to stop hurting or to even get to where you *want* to forgive the other person. And that's okay.

Second, forgiving someone doesn't mean that what they did wasn't wrong or that they even deserve to be forgiven. That part doesn't matter; we need to forgive them because it's the right thing to do.

Third, if you're having trouble forgiving someone, ask God to help you. You might ask Him to help you even *want* to forgive them. That's a start. Ask Him for help. He'll give it to you.

Fourth, forgiving someone doesn't mean you still have to hang out with them. If they continue to treat you badly, maybe it's time to find some different friends.

PS: If someone is bullying you or abusing you in any way, you need to stay away from that person and you need to tell an adult about what's going on. You deserve to be treated well by everyone in your life.

47 **Get Outside**

"What do you mean get outside?" you might ask. "I get outside all the time! I walk to school; I play out in my backyard, and I spend all of recess outside even if it's raining." That's great, but I'm talking about getting outside on purpose. On Saturday, why not take a trip to the park and play on the equipment? See if your family will go on a hike to a spot you've never been before. Explore the forest with your parents or a group and discover some new plants, bugs, or animals you've never seen.

Take a bike ride out in your neighborhood.

Go for a walk around your neighborhood.

Being outside in the sunshine is really good for your body, your feelings, and even your mood. Of course, all these activities are great during the summer when it's warm and dry or if you live in a place that's sunny all the time, like Florida or California. But even in the wintertime you can still go outside and build a snowman or create snow angels. Why not make a couple of snow forts with your friends and have a giant snowball fight?

And if it's raining, get all bundled up, grab a raincoat, some rain boots, and an umbrella, and go for a walk complete with puddle jumping. Then come home, dry off, and have a nice steaming cup of hot chocolate.

Getting outside is a great way to get more energy and exercise and to sharpen your brain.

So, get outside!

What are some fun activities you do (or would like to do) while you're outside?

Discover Your Imagination

Did you know your imagination is a gift God gave you? But it's something you need to develop, just like any good habit. "How do I do that?" you might ask. Good question. Here are a few things you can do to make your imagination strong, creative, and amazing:

1. The number one way to grow your imagination is to spend some time dreaming every day. Probably not during class. Maybe after school or before bed or even for just a couple minutes when you wake up. Ask yourself some fun questions, like *What would I do with ten million dollars? If I could have any job in the world, what would it be? Creating cartoons? Flying jets? Designing clothes? Working with animals?* Other creative questions could be *If I were the president, what's the first thing I'd do? If I could design my dream house, what would I include in it? If I could invent something, what would it be?* Let your imagination go wild and make up some more questions on your own.

2. When you've got some free time, maybe on a rainy day, grab some paper and write a story. It might be about you or a friend or even some pets you know. Make it really funny or serious or mysterious; after all, you're the author—it's totally up to you! Writing fun

stories is a great way to build your imagination.

3. Try drawing a picture to illustrate your story. Or draw the picture first and make up a story to go along with it. "But I can't draw!" you might say. Doesn't matter, just do your best. Check out the next section for some simple tips on how to draw.

4. If you're into sports, try making up your own new game. Maybe it'll be a mash-up of basketball, soccer, and swimming! See, there's no limit when you start to use your imagination!

Developing your creativity is something that will pay off for your whole life. So, get going and start dreaming!

Tips on How to Draw

Drawing is a fun and easy way to discover your imagination. Here are some tips for drawing people and a couple pets!

Everyone (even adults) can draw a stick person. But here's a quick way to turn your stick person into a cartoon.

Draw a stick man. Okay, good. But think about it—have you ever seen anyone walking down the street with their arms and legs sticking out this way? Didn't think so. So, let's have their arms hang down like a normal person. And straighten out their legs so they go down to the ground. Much better.

Now draw parallel lines along the body, legs, and arms to fill them out and give them a body.

Now draw some hands and feet. Add hair and some clothes and there you have it—a cartoon person!

Now try the same trick for drawing a girl. Easy, right?

To draw a cat, just start with a circle. Add some pointy ears and a nose, which looks like a lollipop. Add whiskers and eyes. For the body, draw two halves of a heart. Add the tail, and there you have it! Meow!

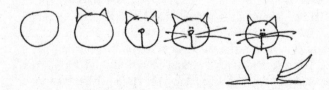

To draw a dog, start with a circle again. Add a half circle on top. Add ears, a nose, and a couple small circles for eyes. Add the body and you've got a cartoon dog.

What else would you like to draw?

# Use Good Table Manners

Your parents have probably taught you how to behave at the dinner table, but here are a few reminders that will make you shine the next time you sit down for a meal:

1. Make sure you show up at the table with clean hands and a clean face. Before you come to dinner, stop by the bathroom and wash your hands really well. Check to make sure you don't have dirt, mud, or leftover food from lunch on your face. That way you'll look great when you sit down.

2. When you sit down, put your napkin in your lap.

3. Wait until everybody is sitting down before you start eating. This is a nice courtesy and helps make sure everyone starts eating at the same time.

4. And if your family says a blessing before the meal, don't start eating before someone prays. Praying before you eat is a good reminder that God supplies our food, and we should be thankful for it. You'll learn how to pray for your meal a little later (see chapter 76).

5. Keep your elbows off the table, and sit up as straight as you can.

6. Make sure you chew with your mouth closed; nobody wants to see what you're eating. Ew. Also, don't talk

with your mouth full. Wait until you swallow before you start talking. We'll wait.

7. Remember your manners. When you ask for more potatoes, beans, peas, or dessert, make sure you say "Please" and "Thank you."

When you use good manners at the table, all the grown-ups who see you will be really impressed. They'll say stuff to your parents like "Your kid is so amazing." And all just because you didn't talk with your mouth full. See how easy it is to make a good impression?

 # Be Flexible

"What does it mean to be flexible?" you might ask. "Do you mean being able to bend over backward or do a somersault?" No, but those are good things to know. Being flexible simply means to learn to be okay when things in your life don't go exactly according to your plans. Learning how to be flexible is something that will help you your whole life.

Let's face it, life is full of surprises, and there are lots of things we can't control. So, it's really good to learn to be flexible and not let things bother you too much.

Here's an example: Let's say you're planning on having some friends over to sleep outside on a warm summer's night. You've got sleeping bags, bug spray, a flashlight, and some yummy snacks. But then something unexpected happens. It starts raining! Now you might get mad or cry or let the rain absolutely ruin your fun time.

OR

You could be flexible. You could run inside and do the whole thing in your living room. After all, you've still got your flashlight, sleeping bags, and snacks, so why not do your *outside* sleepover *inside* where it's warm and dry? If you think like that when unexpected stuff happens, you're being flexible.

Here's another example: Maybe you strike out in your softball game. Nobody likes that. But instead of getting really mad or sad, why not change your thinking and tell yourself, *I better practice my batting so that the next time I'm up maybe I'll hit a home run.* Then get some tips from your coach and practice, practice, practice. And who knows? Your next at bat might just be a homer!

Being flexible just means you don't let the things that are out of your control, control you and your feelings. Being flexible is a great thing to learn no matter how old you are!

Finding His Way Back Home

The son who left home, or the prodigal son, has finally come to his senses and wants to go back to his father. Will you help him find his way back home? Then check out his story in Luke 15:11–32.

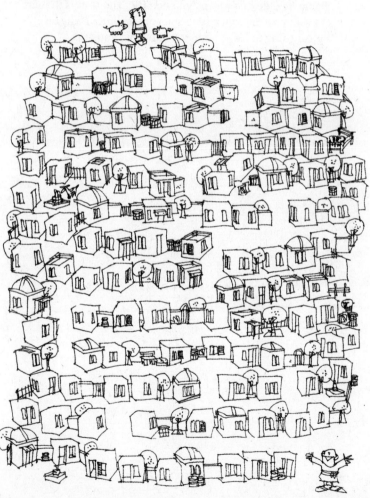

 **Honor Your Parents**

In the Old Testament book of Exodus, God gave His people Ten Commandments—ten things we should do to have a good and blessed life. The very first one is to make sure God is our number one focus. When you think of Him as a friend or even a really good Father, you'll want to obey Him and get to know Him. Other commandments tell us not to lie, steal, or kill anybody, but God also says we're to honor our parents. "Wow! What does that mean?" you ask.

Well, most of us have amazing parents who love us, take care of us, and teach us stuff. So, what are some of the ways we can honor them?

We can listen to them and obey them. If they tell us not to do something, it's because they care about us and want us to be safe. For example, when you were little, they might have said not to run into the street. They were telling you that to keep you safe. So, it's a good thing to listen to them. But as you get older, your parents might say things like "I'm not sure that new friend is the best for you; he might be persuading you to do bad stuff" or "Looks like you need to improve in your spelling." When they say they want you to make good choices, it's good to listen to them because they love you and want the best for you.

Another way to honor your parents is to let them know *how you're doing*. Keeping secrets from them isn't a good idea. Even if you don't believe it sometimes, your parents want you to have a great life. So, if you're having a hard time at school with friends or certain subjects or if you're being bullied, let them know. Talking openly with your parents is a great way to grow and start to understand things about yourself and the world around you.

One more way to honor your parents is to speak respectfully to them. In chapters 23–24, you learned how to guard your mouth. It's especially important to speak respectfully to your parents or teachers or leaders or anyone older than you for that matter. Speaking respectfully to older people is a great way to honor them and learn the most from them.

Learn to Trust God

"Learn to trust God? How do I do that?" you might ask. "I can't see Him, I've never heard His voice, and He lives in heaven! How do I learn to trust Him?"

One way that God wants us to learn to trust Him is by *remembering*—remembering all the good things He's already done for us. Think back. Have you ever had a problem that you never thought would work out? Maybe it was a problem with a friend or a brother or a sister. Maybe you had a subject in school that you thought you'd never understand. But now you look back and see that things worked out just fine. You didn't lose a friend or get stuck in that subject forever. You figured it out.

Well, guess what? God was the One who helped you through that problem in the past, and the good news is He'll be there to help you the next time you have a problem.

When Jesus was here, He told people to ask God for things and to believe they'd already received them. Of course, they have to be things that will be good for you, but believing that you've received the answer to your prayers is a great way to start trusting God.

Sometimes trusting God is doing the thing you know is right even though it might not feel good at the time. Maybe your friends want to do something you know isn't good, or you want to hurt someone who's hurt you. But when you do the right thing, you're trusting God. And believe it or not, it will get easier every time you trust Him.

Trusting God is hard sometimes. But He really wants us to learn how to do that. After all, that's part of growing in your friendship with Him.

God always has your best in mind. He wants you to get to know Him and trust Him in order to have an awesome life.

Choose Good Friends

Choosing good friends is a really important thing to learn now while you're a kid. It's something that will help you all through your life. Having good friends you can trust is a great way to have a good life. When you're young and going to school, most of your friends are probably in your class. Or you might meet some friends in a sports team, scouts, an art class, or a music group. Usually, your best friends are ones who like the same things you do—soccer, playing the trumpet, drawing pictures, being funny, or loving math.

Hopefully you've got some kids in your neighborhood you can hang out with too.

But you'll discover as you go through your life that some friends, though fun and cool, will come and go, while others stick around for a long time. It's important to make sure that the kids you spend the most time with are good for you. Here are a few things you might look for in a good friend:

- *Are they loyal?* If they have plans with you, do they break them at the last minute and go off with someone else? That's not a good habit. Do they talk mean about you when you're not there, or do they stick up for you around others? You want a friend who is loyal to you.
- *Are they honest?* Can you believe what they tell you? Honesty in any friendship is really important. If they

tell you something, you want to be sure it's true. And make sure you're honest with them!

- *Do they make good decisions?* Do they do things that get them in trouble, like fighting, cheating, stealing, or bullying other kids? You might want to stay away from kids like that.

- *Do they tempt* you *to make bad decisions?* Sometimes it's easy as a kid to get influenced by others who want you to join in with stuff that gets you and all of them in trouble. You might be a nice, smart kid but hanging around bad decision-makers might make you a bad decision-maker too. You don't want that.

Of course, nobody is perfect, but when you start to see some things in your friends' lives that aren't so good and aren't making you a better person, you might think about changing your friends. Ask God to give you good friends!

Treasure Your Good Friends

Friends are really important because God created us to live together with people in community. Now, there are kids you might know a little bit, like from class or a team; then there are others you like to hang out with. You're a little bit closer to them. And then there are the kids who are really special in your life, you know, the close friends that come along once in a while. They're the ones you can talk to about anything. You can laugh together and talk about the stuff you love and the stuff that scares you. You can share with them if you've got problems at home or you're not doing well in school. Or if you're lonely, sad, or anxious. These are really special friends. And chances are they feel the same way about you.

Make sure you treat these special friends . . . well, special. Here are some things you can do to make sure you treasure these good friends God has brought into your life:

1. *Make sure their secrets are safe with you.* If they tell you something they don't want anyone to know, make sure you keep it to yourself. Nothing can ruin a friendship quicker than when a secret is shared that was supposed to be kept quiet. Of course, if they share something about them being abused or wanting to hurt themselves or someone else, you need to share that with an adult.

2. *Listen, don't just talk.* A good friendship goes both ways. Make sure you share stuff with them, but make sure they feel safe sharing with you too. Keep the friendship even.

3. *Reach out.* This means don't wait for them to contact you all the time. Find them at school or church, and see how they're doing. Give them a call or a text. Let them know you're thinking about them.

4. *Let them decide what they want to do occasionally.* If you want to play video games but they'd rather go outside and play touch football, go play outside with them. If they'd like to watch a movie, let them choose it. Think of them before yourself.

Be a loyal friend. Stand up for them with others. In your words and actions, stick by them. That's what good friends do. If you follow some of these simple suggestions, you'll honor and treasure your good friends. And who knows? Maybe you'll end up becoming friends for life!

55 Check Out Your Family Tree

Researching your ancestors can be a fun activity for you and your family to do together some rainy weekend.

Find out what country your family is originally from. Learn about that country. Find out who some of your ancestors are. Who knows? You might be related to a king or queen or maybe even some famous person like George Washington or Cleopatra.

"So how do I do that?" you might ask. There are a few ways. Some are quite simple.

Probably the easiest way to start researching your family background is to talk to some of your relatives. If your grandma or grandpa or even great grandparents are around, ask them about their history.

Where did they grow up?

What was it like to live back then?

What was their neighborhood like?

Their school?

Their friends?

What was their first job?

Those kinds of things. Ask them about *their* grandparents. Whoa, depending on their age, some of their grandparents might go back to the Civil War!

If your grandparents live in another part of the country, give them a call or Facetime with them. Or you could send them an email with some of the questions we just mentioned. By doing so, you might find out a lot about your ancestors!

Another way to research your ancestors is to go to an online company such as Ancestry, Family Search, or Myheritage.com. These companies specialize in helping you trace your roots. You and your parents could have a fun time together tracking down your family's history.

 # Ask for Help When You Need It

When you were a little kid, you probably asked for help a lot: "Would you help me reach the top shelf?" "Will you help me tie my shoes?" "Will you help me carry this?"

But now that you're a little older, there are lots of things you can do for yourself. In fact, this book has a lot of things you can learn to do as you grow up. But did you know that it's not only okay but also really good to ask for help when you need it?

Everyone (even adults) needs help once in a while, but if you don't ask, chances are you might miss out on something really cool!

But why don't we ask for help sometimes when we need it? Here are a couple reasons:

1. We might feel embarrassed to ask. We're afraid some-one will think we're not cool if we can't do something for ourselves. Sometimes we might be too proud to admit we need help. But often when we do ask, we learn how to do whatever it is we needed help with and will be able to do it ourselves the next time. There's no problem with asking for help. Besides, once we get good at something, we might be able to help someone else do it later on—*if* they ask.

2. Sometimes as we grow up, we might want to be independent (which just means we don't need

anybody's help), but God made us to need each other. Have you ever noticed that some people—old and young—are really good at some things but need help in other things? Someone who's great with arithmetic or spelling might need help mowing the lawn or shooting a basket. We can all help one another—God made us that way!

So never be afraid to ask for help with what you're doing. None of us are perfect, and all of us can use a little help occasionally. Just ask!

Ask God to Help You . . . Even in the Little Things

Lots of people—maybe even you—believe in God and love and follow Him but think He's so ginormous and huge that He has much more important things to do than answer your prayers. I mean, think about it. There are wars and earthquakes and diseases all over the world. There are kings and presidents and world leaders, and surely they have important stuff going on that God's got to deal with. So why should you believe that God cares about your spelling test on Friday or your baseball game on Saturday? Why would He care if your parents aren't getting along or if you've got a headache or if you're feeling lonely?

But the good news is . . . He does! He cares about all that stuff!

The cool thing about God is that He's, well . . . GOD. And even though He's so big He spoke the entire universe into existence, He's also so amazing that He can see, know, and understand every single one of us. He cares about how you're doing in school, how you're getting along with your brother or sister, and even what you had for breakfast. And you know what? He loves it when we include Him in everything we do.

Are you nervous about a test coming up in school? Ask Him for help (and study for it, of course). Are you excited about a trip to the park or a football game? Let Him know. Are you feeling happy or confident? Tell Him about it.

And if you're having trouble with something—learning to ride your bike or doing your chores—ask Him to help you.

Not only will He do it, but you'll be making Him really happy because your friendship with Him will grow stronger. So, never be afraid to ask God for help on the BIG things *and* the little things!

You might never have thought about asking God to help you with things going on in your life. But He loves it when you do!

1. Why do you think a lot of people think God must be too busy to help them out?

2. Have you ever asked God for help? What was it? How did He help you?

3. Why do you think God likes it when we ask Him for help?

Enjoy Boredom

"What? Nobody likes being bored! How can you enjoy it?" you might ask. Nowadays we don't have to be bored very often; after all we've got books, movies, TV shows, videos, computers, and cell phones around us all the time. We can watch anything we want any*time* we want! And a lot of the technologies and media we have at our fingertips are good and helpful. But God created us to have dreams, ideas, and an active imagination. And when somebody else is entertaining us all the time, we might get lazy and never come up with any creative ideas of our own. So, once or twice a week—unplug! Here's a list of some things you might do on your own without a screen:

Try drawing a superhero body under a photo of your face. What kind of superhero would you be? What would be your superpowers? Flying? Time travel? Being invisible? (Guess that would be hard to draw).

Go for a walk in the woods near your house. Or on the beach or in a park near you. Count how many different birds and animals you see.

Create a miniature golf course through your house on a rainy day. Make holes out of cardboard or plastic cups laid on their sides. Use a real putter. If you don't have one, use a bat or broom to hit the ball.

Go indoor bowling with a beach ball and several liter-size plastic bottles. Set them up in a triangle just like a real bowling alley, and then knock them down with the beach ball.

Grab some paper and draw a picture of your perfect house. Does it have a basketball court? Swimming pool? Horse barn? The sky's the limit!

Spend some time thinking about this: If you could live at any time in history, when would it be? During the Revolutionary War? In the Old West? Back in Jesus's time? What job would you have back then?

Now it's your turn! Come up with two or three ideas of fun stuff to do on your own.

59 Memorize God's Word

As we talked about before, the Bible is a really special book. After all, God wrote it Himself (through about 40 of His people). But when it comes to memorizing it, you might think, *No way! How do I do that? Where do I even start?* Well, memorizing Scripture (that's what you call the verses in the Bible) is just like everything else you want to learn. Start small. Don't feel like you've got to memorize the entire book of Genesis to start off with, but how about one verse? How about the very first line in the Old Testament?

In the beginning God created the heavens and the earth. (Gen. 1:1 NIV)

That's not so hard, is it? Let's try another couple of easy ones:

Love one another. (1 John 3:23 NIV)

Jesus Christ is the same yesterday, today, and forever. (Heb. 13:8)

These are just a few of the many, many verses in the Bible you can start with when you want to memorize Scripture.

Why is it important to memorize God's Word? Because having it in your mind will help you when you come upon a tough situation. When you feel confused, upset, or discouraged, bring

God's Word to mind, and it'll strengthen, encourage, and instruct you.

Here are just a few examples:

- Are you afraid? "When I am afraid, I will trust you" (Ps. 56:3).
- Are you lonely? "I [God] will never leave you; I will never abandon you" (Heb. 13:5).
- Are you tempted to do something bad? "Stay awake and pray for strength against temptation" (Matt. 26:41).
- Are you discouraged? "Why am I so sad? Why am I so upset? I should put my hope in God" (Ps. 42:11).

See? It's fun, challenging, and easy to "hide" God's Word in your heart (see Ps. 119:11 NIV). You'll be glad you did!

Hearing from God

God wants us to get to know Him, and one way we can do that is by reading and memorizing His Word, the Bible. See how many of the words from the list you can find in the word search.

```
F  N  I  C  E  K  D  N  J  U  F  S  E
G  A  A  G  E  E  V  L  U  U  H  C  J
U  M  N  L  T  M  K  U  U  S  T  R  U
I  E  B  A  O  A  A  K  A  T  O  I  A
E  I  L  V  E  R  S  E  H  L  C  P  C
B  A  I  P  I  K  D  B  T  I  I  T  T
T  E  S  T  A  M  E  N  T  A  M  U  I
J  D  T  J  Z  H  H  L  D  S  A  R  W
B  Q  E  P  G  O  S  P  E  L  Q  E  C
G  D  N  R  J  E  T  Q  O  T  O  A  R
J  U  M  A  T  T  H  E  W  O  R  D  U
A  Q  A  Y  S  U  G  L  P  Q  Z  R  A
T  I  Z  M  C  G  A  F  D  B  M  I  A
```

BIBLE	MARK	SPEAK
GOSPEL	MATTHEW	TESTAMENT
JOHN	NAME	VERSE
LISTEN	PRAY	WORD
LORD	READ	
LUKE	SCRIPTURE	

 # Balance Confidence with Humility

We all know what confidence is. That's when you feel certain and able to do something. You might be really good at swimming. Or spelling or drawing or dancing or making things. That's confidence, and that's a great thing to have. In fact, it's good to feel confident when you try something new, whether it's playing softball, baking cookies, or teaching a little kid how to ride a bike.

But it's also good to develop humility. "Humility? What's that?" you might ask. Humility is being able to be thankful for all the gifts and talents you have without becoming braggy or self-centered about it. We've all known people who can do something well and they let *everybody* know about it. It's kind of a "Look at me! Aren't I great?" attitude. And we've all been around humble people. They might be really good at something, but they don't make a big deal about it.

When you think about it, anything you do well is a gift or talent that comes from God. After all, all the good stuff in our lives comes from Him, doesn't it?

So, how do you combine these two things—confidence and humility?

It's important to feel confident, to feel like you're going to succeed. But when you do—succeed, that is—make sure you remember who helped you do it. Like I said earlier, whenever we do something well, it's because God gave us the ability, skill, and talent to do it.

When you realize that God is the One behind all our successes, it's easy to remain humble. Let people know that God helped you in whatever it was you succeeded at. Sports, art, music, even training your dog. And also give other people the credit. That's a great way to be humble. Do these things, and in a funny way, you'll have even more confidence the next time you try something!

Work Hard. Play Hard. Rest Hard.

As you continue to grow up and discover new things, this is a good motto to live by: Work Hard. Play Hard. Rest Hard. Let's look at work, play, and rest and see how they work together.

1. *Work hard.* This is a good idea no matter what kind of work you do. Schoolwork, chores, or even something you get paid for. When you're in class or doing your homework, learn to do your best and try to do a great job. Is one of your jobs putting out the trash? Do it without even being asked. Do you have reading or math due tomorrow? Don't rush through it. Make sure you take your time, then double check to make sure they're all perfect. Do you mow a neighbor's lawn for money? Do an excellent job. Don't skip the corners, and make sure you pick up all the grass and get rid of it. Get the idea? Work hard!

2. *Play hard.* Even if you're not on an official team, do your best to play hard. Give it your all. If you're on an organized team with a coach and their helpers, listen to them. Do what they suggest. After all, they're older, and they've been through this before. But no matter where you play—with friends in your neighborhood, with your family, or even with your dog—go for it! Play hard!

3. *Rest hard.* This means know what it means to take a break every once in a while. Make sure you go to bed at the best time for you to get a good night's sleep. Check out chapter 11 for more tips on sleep. Make sure you take a day off a week, like Sunday where you can rest, relax, and recharge. We need to make sure we're always taking breaks so we can restore our energy. Rest hard!

Our bodies were made to work hard, play hard, and rest hard. If you do these three things, you're going to be set up for success!

Fun Fact: In God's original Ten Commandments in the Old Testament, He talks more about taking a Sabbath or rest than He does stealing or killing. God takes rest pretty seriously, and so should we.

Stay Connected

It's good, no it's great, to have all kinds of different friends. Kids who like sports and kids who don't. Kids who look like you and kids who are way different. Kids who love God and kids who don't . . . yet. In fact, God wants us to be friends with all kinds of people. After all, how else will they get to know about Jesus and how much God loves them?

But it's also important that you hang out with kids and adults who love God and are growing in their friendship with Him.

In fact, Jesus said that He's like a vine and we're the branches (see John 15). We need to make sure we're connected to the vine, so we'll keep growing and getting closer to Him every day. What happens to a branch that's been cut off from the tree? Right, it gets all dried out and can no longer grow. You don't want to be that branch!

So, the best way to keep growing in your friendship with God is by being around others who are also part of the vine—Jesus.

Think of it this way. When we hang out with our Christian friends, it's like we're coming back to the base camp after a big mountain climb. We can go off and explore, climb, and even challenge ourselves, but we need to always come back to base camp to get fed, rested up, and be encouraged to go out and try big things again.

Base camp for you might be church or Sunday school or some Christian friends you know from school or the neighborhood.

God created us to be close to other Jesus followers so that we can encourage one another, learn from one another, and build one another up. It doesn't mean you'll need to be serious all the time—sometimes you'll laugh your heads off—but it's good to know that these friends know you well and that they've got your back when you need it.

So, make sure you stay connected—to God through Jesus and to other people who love God just like you!

 # Don't Get Sunburned

Here's another way you can take care of yourself and stay healthy, and it's really easy: Take care of your skin! Before you go outside to play or just hang out, remember to do one thing: Apply sunscreen! Easy, right?

Even though it's fun to be out on a warm, sunny day, it's important to make sure you're not getting too much sun. Here are a couple reasons for that:

1. You don't ever want to get a sunburn. Nothing can spoil a fun day at the beach or at the park like having a painful sunburn. Trust me, it's not fun to hurt all over. So put on sunscreen before you go out, then go have fun. Sunscreen = no sunburn. And after a few hours or if you go swimming, make sure you put some more on to make sure you're covered.

2. If you spend lots of time outside without sunscreen when you're young, your skin might not like it. You don't want your skin to get all old looking when you get older—like twenty.

So, remember when you go outside on a sunny day, make sure you either rub on or spray on some sunscreen. You'll be glad you did.

"What if it's all cloudy outside?" you might ask. "I probably don't need sunscreen then, right?" Wrong. Even on a cloudy day, make sure you put it on. Just because you can't see the sun up in the sky doesn't mean it's not there. In fact, sometimes cloudy and snowy days are even worse for sunburn than warm, sunny days. So, play it safe—put on that sunscreen!

DID YOU KNOW?

A group of kittens is called a kindle.
A group of owls is called a parliament.
A group of rhinos is called a crash.
A group of whales is called a pod.
A group of coyotes is called a band.
A group of rattlesnakes is called a rhumba.

Learn How to Use Simple Tools

Even as a kid, boys and girls can learn how to safely use some tools. Of course, you might want to make sure your dad or mom are right there to show you how they work and what they do. Here are a few tools you might use to fix little things around the house:

Hammer—This is probably the most basic tool you'll ever use. Most of the time, you'll be using a hammer to hit nails. So, if you want to practice a little bit, why not have your mom get a piece of wood about a foot long (see the next tool for tips on

measuring) and a couple nails. Practice holding the
nail up and tap it gently until it sticks in the wood.
Once it's standing on its own, you can hit it a little
harder—not too hard—and make sure your fingers are
out of the way. After a little practice, you'll get to be a
pro at hammering a nail. Make sure you only hammer
nails into your piece of wood though, not anywhere
you're not supposed to.

Measuring tape or tape measure—These are fun and really easy
to use. Hold up the measuring tape next to the thing you
want to measure—like your piece of wood or yourself. (You
do want to know how tall you are, don't you?). Make
sure the tape is straight, and then check the
number next to the end of what you
want to measure like in the picture.
You can measure almost anything—
your dresser, your bed, and even your
little brother. If he's okay with that.

Screwdriver—You can practice with a screwdriver with anything that has a screw in it. Again, make sure your mom
or dad are with you to show you a safe screw to work
on. Don't ever work around an electric socket where
you plug stuff in. That can be dangerous. Screwdriv-
ers are really helpful when you need to tighten or
loosen a screw.

Pliers—Pliers are another easy and simple-to-use
tool. You usually use pliers when something is too tight to

open with your fingers. Just open them up and put them around whatever it is you want to loosen. Squeeze the handle to make sure it's tight and then turn. Usually, you'll want to turn toward the left to loosen something and toward the right to tighten it. A great way to remember is to say, "Lefty loosey, righty tighty."

Be Safe Online

Depending on how old you are, chances are you probably spend some time online on your computer. Computers are amazing. You can find information you might need for school. You can find out things that are going on in your town or around the world in places like India or Peru. And of course, there are tons of games you can play too. But just like anything, there are some things you need to do to protect yourself when you're online.

You've probably heard this before, but never give any personal information about where you live, where you go to

school, or even your full name to someone you don't know. There are some bad guys out there that would love to get your information and rip you off. I mean, think about it this way. If you were out on the street and some totally random person came up to you and asked who you were, where you lived, and what school you went to, you wouldn't tell them, would you? That would be silly. So be smart online too.

Also don't get caught in the garbage can of stinky stuff online. There are things out there that nobody needs to see, especially kids. Things that involve sex and bad language and violence that aren't helpful at all in making you a great person and helping you have a great life. If you come across stuff like that accidentally—just click off right away. Also tell your parents about it.

Just to be safe, you might even ask your parents to put some filters on your internet so you won't get stuff online that you don't want to see.

Plant a Flower or Vegetable

You might live on a farm with tons of space to grow things, like apples, filberts, or peaches. Or you might live in an apartment with a balcony and three pots of flowers. Either way, working outside in a garden can be a fun and interesting way to learn new things. It's amazing how God designed plants, flowers, fruits, and vegetables to grow. And you can be a part of the process!

First you take a little seed. No matter what you're growing, it usually starts with a seed. You can get those at a nursery or a home improvement store. When you get home, take them out of the packet, dig a little hole in the ground or the pot, and plant them.

Next, your little seed will need water and most of the time plenty of sunshine, depending on what you planted. The seed packet will usually tell you what the plant needs.

As time goes on, you might need to come and rake leaves and the dead stuff away from your little plant. Some weeds might have sprouted up, and you'll need to pull them out. Make sure you get the roots of the weeds, so they won't come back. And make sure your plant gets watered regularly, either from the rain or, in drier months, with your hose or watering can.

After a while, your seeds will start to sprout above the ground. Soon they'll grow and, depending on what you planted, they might get really big and green. They might even start to grow fruit or vegetables!

The more you learn to work in the garden, the more fun you'll have as you start to grow your own tomatoes, pumpkins, green beans, or broccoli. Look at that, you're growing your own food!

 **Get Organized**

Have you ever spent an hour looking for some homework, a T-shirt, a sports uniform, or a soccer ball? It's frustrating to lose something and not know where you left it. Getting organized isn't just for grown-ups. It's really helpful no matter how old you are! And it's not hard. If you keep up with it every day, you'll be on top of things and probably won't lose stuff again. Here are some ways you can start to get your life organized:

- *Create a place for your important stuff.* It could be a box, a cubby, or a basket. Keep things in there like school papers for tomorrow, permission slips, homework, and maybe even your glasses and shoes. If you always put stuff in the same place, you'll always know where it is.

- *Clean out your backpack!* Once a week, go through your backpack and get rid of the things you don't need. Old school papers, books you don't need now, and maybe even your lunch from two weeks ago. Ew! You don't want your backpack to smell like old brown bananas.

- *Make lists.* When you've got chores around the house or even homework for school, write down everything you need to do. When you write things down, you can

174

always go back and see if you're remembering to do the things you need to. Feed the dog? Rake the leaves? Do your reading assignment? Once you do that task, check it off your list. That's a great way to be organized and not forget to do something!

Can you think of other ways you can get organized?

 **Read for Fun**

Do you like to read? Wow, come to think of it, you're reading right now! Good job! What kind of books do you like to read? Books with lots of pictures? Adventures or mysteries? Do you like books about animals? Or if you really want to be honest, do you *not* like to read or have trouble doing it? If you have trouble reading, that's okay. Most people had to learn how to read at some point, and some people are faster than others at picking it up. If it's taking you awhile to learn, no sweat; just keep at it and you'll get better and better all the time. If you're really having trouble reading, tell your mom or dad or even your teacher. They'll help you learn so you can begin to discover the amazing world of books.

Right now, the only reading you might do is for school. But as you get more and more used to it, there are all kinds of cool books out there you can read for fun. And by reading, you can learn about pretty much anything in the world.

There are picture books with cool illustrations that help tell the story.

There are chapter books that are especially written for kids who are just learning to read. And chapter books have cool stories, some about kids just like you.

As you get older there are other kinds of books including graphic novels that use art and words to tell exciting stories. Did you know there are even graphic novel Bibles for kids?

By reading you can end up in exotic places like India or South Africa or Mars or Venus! You'll meet exciting people like Abraham Lincoln, Martin Luther King Jr., or Darth Vader.

And if you have a public library in your town, go check it out. Libraries are cool places that have hundreds of books, games, magazines, movies, and sometimes even video games that you can borrow for free. Plan a visit to your local library soon—you'll be glad you did.

Reading is something you'll be able to enjoy all your life.

 **Write a Note**

Chances are you're learning how to write or print in school, or maybe you learned that a long time ago. Well, writing a note is a great way to practice your writing and at the same time do something nice for someone. I've even included a couple sample notes in this chapter.

"Why should I write a note?" you might ask. Well, there are several good reasons:

1. You might want to thank someone for a gift or a nice thing they did for you. Did your grandma send you a gift for your birthday? Did your best friend's family take you camping last week? Writing a thank-you note is a great way to let them know how much you appreciate what they did. Check out the sample thank-you note.

2. You can write a note to someone you haven't seen in a while. Everybody loves to get a handwritten note in the mail from time to time. Has it been awhile since you've seen your cousin? Did a good friend move to another city? Write a note to let them know you are thinking about them. Wouldn't you like to get a note like that? Wouldn't that make you feel special? Check out the sample friend note.

3. You can send a note for no reason! Just let somebody—a friend, an aunt, an uncle, or a grandparent—know they are on your mind.

4. You might buy some note cards at the store, or even better, grab a piece of paper and draw a picture on one side and write your note on the other side. Then get an envelope, find the person's address (you might need a parent to help with that), put a stamp on it, and mail it off. I guarantee the person receiving your note will love it!

Sample Thank-You Note

Dear Aunt Mary,

I just wanted to say THANK YOU for the awesome game you gave me for my birthday. This is my favorite type of game, and I've been playing it a lot. I even had some friends over yesterday, and we played it together. They liked it too.

Thanks for making my birthday so special. You're the best!

Love, Me

Sample Friend Note

Hi Sophia,

I'm just writing to say hi! I was thinking about you and wondering how you were doing.

My family went to the coast last week. It was kind of cold, but we had fun.

School's about the same. What's new with you?

Just wanted to say I miss you! Hope to see you soon.

Me

70 Watch What You Watch!

How many devices are available to you? The TV, a cell phone, a computer? Nowadays, there are so many screens around, and there are some pretty cool things to watch. But not everything that's out there is good for you. There are some movies that contain a lot of grown-up stuff, violence, and bad language, and they won't be helpful to you as you grow.

Sometimes it's hard to avoid bad language or scary scenes in a TV show or movie, but you don't want to make a habit of watching these kinds of shows. Most people would say kids shouldn't be watching stuff like that. But when you think about it, it's not really helpful for anybody, no matter what their age. I mean, think of it this way. If you saw a sandwich laying in the middle of the sewer, you wouldn't pick it up and eat it, would you? Hope not! Watching stuff on TV or online that's not good for you is like eating a sandwich that's been sitting in the sewer.

So how can you stay away from TV or online content that's not good for you? Whew. That's a good question.

First, the most important thing to do is to ask God to help you. "What? God will help me watch what I watch?" you might ask. Absolutely. He wants you to watch good and safe things even more than you do. Go ahead and ask Him. Just say, "Lord, would You help me stay away from watching stuff that's not good for me?"

Chances are your parents want you to watch things that are right for your age, too, so you might make sure you only tune into a screen when one of them is nearby.

Be smart. If you feel a little guilty watching something, chances are that might be God nudging you to switch to something else.

If you have trouble staying away from stuff online that you know isn't good for you, let someone know. They'll help you watch what you watch!

There are so many choices of things to watch out there, but not all of them are good for you. Talk about how you can watch shows that build you up.

1. Why do you think some shows just aren't good for a kid to watch?

2. What are some ways you can help each other find good things to watch on TV or online?

3. When you watch something that builds you up, you feel good, don't you? Talk about a good thing you've watched recently.

 # Know How to Be Found

This could also be titled "Know *What to Do* if You Get Lost." Or if you get separated from your family at a store or out in public. The first thing to do when you realize your parents or siblings aren't with you is to not worry! Even though it might feel scary, the truth is you and they will get back together soon.

A great way to feel confident and get back together quickly is to figure out a plan ahead of time (like when you're at home and not lost!). The first thing to do is either memorize or write down your mom or dad's cell phone number and always keep it with you.

Here are a few more things you might do if you ever get separated from your parents in a public place:

- Look for a mom who has kids with her. Tell her what happened, and chances are she'll help you get reconnected with your family.
- If you're in a mall or shopping area and you don't see a mom around, go to the information desk or security office and let them know you've gotten separated from your parents. This kind of thing happens all the time. If there's not an information desk, go to a store and speak to one of the workers. They'll have a phone there so you can call your mom's or dad's cell. Remember? You memorized it way back before you got lost.

- If you're out on the street and you get separated from your family, look for a safe place to hang out. A fire station, a library, or a doctor's office are great options. And once again, they can call your parent's cell phone for you and let them know where you are.

Remember, if you get lost, your parents are always going to find you, and you'll be together soon.

Get Ready for Bed— without Being Asked!

Now, some kids *like* to get ready for bed. Maybe they're tired or just ready to wind down and go to sleep. But some kids—and you might be one of them—*hate* going to bed. They like to stay up, watch a little more TV, get another glass of water, or maybe hear one more story. But going to bed and getting enough sleep are really important as you grow (remember chapter 11?). So, what are some things to remember when you get ready for bed?

Figure out a good bedtime that works well for both you and your parents—nine? Nine thirty? Make sure that you set a time that will give you at least nine to twelve hours of sleep before the morning. As you get older, your bedtime might get a little later each year. If you're good about getting to bed at the time you set with your parents, then maybe next school year you might say, "I'm thinking I should start going to bed a half hour later than I've been doing it. What do you say?"

Next, think of the things you need to do before going to bed.

Lay out your clothes for the morning.

Gather the books and schoolwork you'll need tomorrow.

Brush your teeth and wash your face.

Get into your jammies, give your parents a kiss, and snuggle in.

A good way to relax and calm down before going to sleep is by reading a book, and not one on a screen or your phone. Just read a little bit, and pretty soon you'll be ready to sleep.

Getting drowsy? Sweet dreams! Good night, sleep tight!

Learn How to Tell a Joke

Everybody likes to laugh, and a great way to make friends and enjoy conversation is to share a joke or a funny story you know.

"So, how hard is it to tell a joke?" you might ask. It's really not hard, especially if you know these important joke-telling tips:

1. Make sure you include all the most important info as you set up your joke. Sometimes if you leave out an important word or phrase, your joke won't make any sense.

2. Make sure your joke is appropriate and doesn't make fun of anyone. Nobody likes having people laugh at them. It's embarrassing.

3. Most jokes have a rhythm or pace, so it's good to learn the joke word for word. Listen to the difference in these two similar jokes:

   My dad's a magician. He saws people in half.
   Wow, do you have any siblings?
   Two half-sisters and a half-brother.

See? Funny, right? Now look what happens when you don't use the right words:

My father is a magician. One of the tricks he does is sawing people in half.

Wow. Do you have any brothers and sisters?

Yeah. I've got a half-brother and two half-sisters.

Not so funny, right? Just a few words can make a difference. Try to memorize the joke word for word. It'll work much better.

4. Be confident! If you're confident when you tell your joke, your audience, whether it's just a couple friends or an entire auditorium filled with people, will relax and enjoy the story. One way to feel really confident is to memorize your joke.

5. Practice, practice, practice. When you have your joke (or jokes) down so that you could say them in your sleep (not really), you'll feel confident and be able to get a laugh no matter where you are.

6. Have fun! This isn't brain surgery. Telling jokes and making people laugh helps them to relax and enjoy your time together.

Here are a few riddles and one-liners you might use for practice:

Did you hear about the two guys who stole a calendar? They each got six months.

What did one plate say to the other plate? Dinner's on me!

I'd like to get a job cleaning mirrors. It's really something I could see myself doing.

What do you call a polar bear wearing earmuffs? Anything you want. He can't hear you.

What did one elevator say to the other elevator? I think I'm coming down with something.

Why was the math book so sad? Because it had so many problems.

What did one candle say to the other? I'm going out tonight.

Why did the policeman open a bakery? He wanted to make COPcakes.

What has four wheels and honks? A goose on a skateboard.

Help Take Care of a Younger Kid

Now, don't worry, this doesn't mean you're going to raise your younger brother or sister or babysit your neighbor's kids for weeks at a time. But playing with and taking care of a little kid is good practice for you as you grow older. You might even start out by having a parent in the room with you as you take care of a little kid.

And by the way, did you know that little kids think older kids like you are the coolest thing in the world? They look up to you and might even start copying the things you do.

So, what do you do with a younger kid, anyway? Well, start by thinking of some fun things to do with them. Do they want to play with Legos? Go ahead and help them build something. Do they want to look at a book with you? Let them choose one, then read it to them. Do they want to play hide-and-seek? Maybe they'd like to draw a picture. Are they hungry? Cut up an apple or peel a banana for them. Maybe you can make a sandwich for them.

Taking care of a kid who's younger than you is a great way to learn responsibility and help out your mom or a neighbor once in a while.

As you get older, you might be able to start charging for your babysitting services and make some extra money.

What are some ideas of fun things you might do with a younger kid? Be creative. Write them down:

Fun ideas to do with a kid:

 # Realize You're Not Perfect

Throughout this book, we've been talking about doing your very best in everything you do. And that's what you should do. You want people to know that you'll do a good job and follow through on everything they ask of you—schoolwork, chores, even being a good friend. But along with doing your best, kids (and adults!) need to remember that we're only human!

In other words, give yourself a break! There will always be things you can't do really well, or maybe you're just starting out and still have some things to learn. The important thing is that you're trying, and guess what? You're not going to succeed at everything you do. You may not be the best basketball player in the world or the world's greatest artist, dancer, guitar player, or chef. And that's okay.

God created you to be *you*, and He's given you amazing gifts that He didn't give to anyone else. And He wants you to grow in those gifts and use them to make Him shine.

But always remember, God loves you! There's nothing you can do to make Him love you more, and there's nothing you can ever do to make Him love you less! If you can't hit a home run or paint an amazing picture or understand math, He still loves you and He wants you to love yourself.

Now, there are some things you might want to learn how to do but be patient! Nobody can do *everything*. So, whether it's a sport, schoolwork, or learning how to swim, keep trying and practicing and soon you'll get better at whatever it is you're trying to do. Also, as you grow, you'll begin to discover the things you (and God) really want you to do. You'll also discover the things you don't really care about, and that's okay too. That way you'll have more time to focus on the stuff you're really getting good at.

Remember, God loves you so much that just thinking of you makes Him smile. Even if you can't hit a home run.

76 Learn How to Pray for Your Meal

Why do people pray before a meal? Have you ever thought about that? Your family might pray before your meals, or this might be new to you. It's not bad if you don't say grace before you eat, but once you understand why people do it, you might want to start. Here are just a couple reasons it's good to pray before your meal:

1. Whenever you thank God for the food you're about to eat, you're following Jesus's example. Before He fed more than five thousand people with just a few loaves of bread and a couple fish (great story—check it out in Luke 9:10–17), Jesus prayed to His Father and thanked Him for the food. So, when you realize that Jesus prayed before He ate a meal, it seems like a good idea for *us* to do it too.

2. When you pray before a meal, you're thanking God for taking good care of you and giving you good food to eat. Most of us have all the food we need and can eat anytime we want. But all over the world, and even in your own country, there are people who don't have enough food to eat. It's always good to remember the good things God does for us. And thanking Him for the food we're about to eat is a good reminder of all the good things He gives us every day.

"So how do I do it?" you might be asking. "How do I pray for my food? What do I say? Are there certain words I need to use?" Not at all. There are no particular words you need to use. Just be honest with God. You might want to thank Him for all the good stuff you're about to eat. You might thank Him that your mom or dad took the time to make the meal. You might thank God for your family and friends who are sitting around the table with you. And you might ask God to bless your meal and bless the time you have together. And remember, you don't need to pray too long; after all, you don't want the food to get cold!

Try writing a prayer you'd like to say at your next meal:

Succeed at Your Schoolwork

If you attend school, whether you go to a public school, a private school, or you're homeschooled, you might get the idea that there are some kids who are just smart and that school is easy for them. And then there are other kids who struggle with their schoolwork and find it hard. You might find yourself somewhere in between the two. But did you know there are a few things you can do to make your schoolwork not only easier but done in a way that it'll be great? And they're pretty simple. Check these out:

1. First, if you have homework to do, figure out *when* you want to do it. You might say "never," but that's not really a choice. Are you a kid who likes to get right at it when you get home from school? That way, you'll

get it over with, and then you can have a snack and maybe go outside and play. Or you might be a kid who likes to relax and play a little bit right when they get home from school. After all, you've been studying and listening in class all day long; you need a break! That's fine too. Figure out when you work best, and do your schoolwork then.

2. Another good way to make schoolwork a little easier is to have a spot where you usually study. It might be at your desk or the kitchen table or even sitting on your bed. Make sure it's a place where you won't be interrupted and there aren't any distractions like the TV or video game console.

3. Next, before you start working, make sure you have everything you need close at hand—books, pencils, paper, notebook, whatever you need. That way you won't be interrupted in the middle of your study session looking for an eraser.

4. And here's a tip that lots of people use: Do the hardest thing first. "What?" you might ask. "That doesn't sound very fun." But think about it. If math is your hardest subject, do it first while your brain is still sharp and alert. Think of how nice it will feel to get the hard thing done. What a relief!

By the way, one reason you get homework in school is to teach you to work on your own—to manage your time and be a self-starter. These are great skills you'll need to succeed in life.

 **Realize How Much You're Loved**

Did you know that there's one person who loves you more than anything in the whole world? Of course, your mom and dad love you like that, but there's someone else who loves you even more than they do! And you might not know it.

It's God.

It's true! Your idea of God might be that He's a really serious, distant ruler out there in the universe somewhere and that He doesn't even know who you are. Or that He's watching you but only to see if you do anything wrong. And He's not going to be very happy about it. But that's not who God is at all.

Yes, He does know everything about you. What you like and what you don't like. Who your best friend is and how much you love your dog or your cat. He even knows when you don't get along with your brother or sister, and He knows the times you guys are best friends. He looks at you with love in His eyes all day long.

In the Bible, there are lots of times when we hear how God feels about us. Here are just a few:

> *He sings over us.* "He will sing and be joyful about you" (Zeph. 3:17).
>
> *He knows our name.* "Don't be afraid, because I have saved you. I have called you by name, and you are mine" (Isa. 43:1).

He protects us. "He will protect you like a bird spreading its wings over its young. His truth will be like your armor and shield" (Ps. 91:4).

He leads us and teaches us. "I will guide them along paths they have not known. I will make the darkness become light for them" (Isa. 42:16).

He calls us His kids. "The Father has loved us so much! He loved us so much that we are called children of God. And we really are his children" (1 John 3:1).

So, now it's up to you to begin to understand the great love God has for you. And because of that love you can be:

At peace

Confident

Loving to other people

Always remember, God loves you more than you could ever imagine, and He has amazing plans for your life! Jeremiah 29:11 says that God has "good plans for you. I don't plan to hurt you. I plan to give you hope and a good future." God loves you!

TALK IT OVER

Sometimes it's easier to imagine that God is big enough to create the whole universe than it is to believe He loves us and is interested in our lives.

1. How does it make you feel when you hear that God loves you and has plans for your future?

2. What plans do you think God might have for you?

3. If you're with other family members or in a small group, share some of the plans God might have for the other people in your group.

79 Find the Answer in Your Bible

You may think your Bible is kind of old and won't have anything to say about your life today. After all, it was written over two thousand years ago. That's a long time! But since the Bible is God's Word and God is really smart, He understands exactly what you need right when you need it. So, if you're feeling anxious, angry, or lonely, God can speak to you through His Word—the Bible.

Here are just a few examples:

Feeling anxious or scared? "So don't worry, because I am with you. Don't be afraid, because I am your God. I will make you strong and will help you. I will support you with my right hand that saves you" (Isa. 41:10).

Feeling upset? "Why am I so sad? Why am I so upset? I should put my hope in God" (Ps 43:5).

Feeling lonely? "Turn to me and be kind to me. I am lonely and hurting" (Ps. 25:16).

Are you sad? "The Lord is close to the brokenhearted" (Ps. 34:18).

Are you happy? "Be full of joy in the Lord always. I will say again, be full of joy" (Phil. 4:4).

Is someone you know sick? "The Lord will give him strength when he is sick. The Lord will make him well again" (Ps. 41:3).

Does God seem far away? "Where can I go to get away from your Spirit? Where can I run from you?" (Ps. 139:7).

Do you feel guilty? "But if we confess our sins, he will forgive our sins. We can trust God. He does what is right. He will make us clean from all the wrongs we have done" (1 John 1:9).

Whenever you're faced with struggles, go to your Bible and see what God has to say to you. Of course, it's always good to go to someone who's older and who understands the Bible and talk with them too. Who knows? The two of you might just help each other hear what God is saying to you both!

 # Finish Your Task

No matter what your "task" might be—schoolwork, household chores, taking care of a pet—it's important to follow through with the job and finish it well. Sometimes when you're asked to do something, especially if it's something new, you might get excited and start off really well. But as you're working on it for a while, you may begin to lose interest or at least lose your enthusiasm. And then maybe you stop altogether.

But the difference between somebody who does an *okay* job and somebody who's living a great life is that the great life person keeps going until the job is totally finished. For example:

- If you're supposed to rake the backyard, don't just make a pile of leaves in the middle of the grass. Gather them either into bags or into the recycling can. Don't leave them on the lawn.
- If you've got 25 math problems for homework, don't do just 20 of them. Finish up all 25.
- If you make lunch for you and your siblings, make sure you clean up the kitchen when you're done.
- If you're folding your clean clothes from the laundry, make sure you take care of all of them and also put them away in your dresser drawers. That way they'll be all ready for you the next time you need them.

Learning to finish your tasks is an important lesson for everybody as they grow up. That way people will know they can trust you to do an excellent job at everything you do. Plus, you'll feel better knowing you did a good job and finished your task.

Help Out at the Table

Who makes most of the meals around your place? Mom? Dad? Do you and your siblings help out? Well, no matter who's doing the cooking, there are lots of ways you can help with meals, especially dinner. Here are some easy ways to help out when it comes to mealtimes:

1. Help set the table. This means putting a fork, spoon, and knife at everyone's place as well as a napkin.

2. Pour water into everyone's glass. Be careful. If you're using a pitcher, it's probably a good idea to use both hands when you pour.

3. Help bring the food to the table. The cook will be really grateful for extra hands to bring the potatoes, salad, vegetables, and bread over to the table.

4. After the meal, it's helpful to take your plate (and maybe somebody else's too) over to the sink. Ask your mom or dad to show you how to clean off your plate and silverware and put them into the dishwasher if you have one. If not, offer to help them wash dishes a few times a week.

5. Help clear off the other things from the table also, like other plates, serving dishes, or silverware that hasn't been used. When everyone works together to clean up, the task goes faster.

Glass

Napkin

Fork

Knife

Spoon

Learn from Other People's Examples— Good or Bad

Did you know that all around you there are people who are teaching you how to live a good life?

"What? Where are they?" you might ask. "Where are all these people, and how are they teaching me?" Look around you. There are parents, teachers, brothers, sisters, friends at school and church and even people in your town you may not know.

And they're teaching you what to do and what *not* to do every day. Here's how that works.

First, you've got people in your life who give you *good* examples of how to live. These might be your parents or family members or even someone from your neighborhood. Watch how they treat people. Are they kind? Do they use words that build other people up? Are they truthful and honest? Do they do a good job at the things they need to do? Are they reliable and trustworthy? These are the people God's put in your life as *good* examples. These are the people you want to follow and imitate.

Then there are people in your life who aren't such good examples for you to follow. They're not bad people but for some reason they aren't honest. You can't trust what they say. They might get lazy and not do a good job either in school or at their work. You still need to love them but let them be an example you *don't* want to follow. And some of these people even suffer the consequences when they aren't truthful or don't do a good job. You can learn to avoid those consequences by not doing what these people do. See? You can learn from their bad example.

And here's something else to think about. What kind of example are *you*? Do your younger siblings want to be like you, or do they see things they don't want to follow? Hopefully, this book will help you become a good example for others in your family, at school, and in your neighborhood. Let others learn good things from you!

Learn Your Way Around

One cool thing about getting older is you get to be out on your own a little more every year. Of course, if you're six or seven years old, chances are you're not going to go to the mall or hang around downtown by yourself. But it is important for you to learn your way around your neighborhood.

This is a fun thing you can do with either one of your parents or an older brother or sister. Some day when the sun is shining, go on a little field trip around your neighborhood and discover what's out there. Take a walk and learn all the streets around you so you could find your way home if you ever needed to. Is your school close enough to walk to? How about your church? Is there a store or library nearby?

Depending on where you live, there also might be areas that aren't safe to go through, so you should stay away from them.

As you get more and more familiar with your neighborhood, your mom or dad can even let *you* lead the way home sometimes.

When you get home, why not either make a list or draw a picture of the things you discovered as you walked through the neighborhood?

Where is your friend's house?

Where is your school (if it's close by)?

What are some familiar landmarks you can recognize? A blue house? A really tall tree? A grocery store? A certain sign?

As you get to know your neighborhood, you'll start to become more confident. And if you ever for some reason end up away from where you live, you'll always know how to get back.

And who knows? Someday maybe you'll take your little brother or sister on the same walk, so they can learn about the neighborhood too!

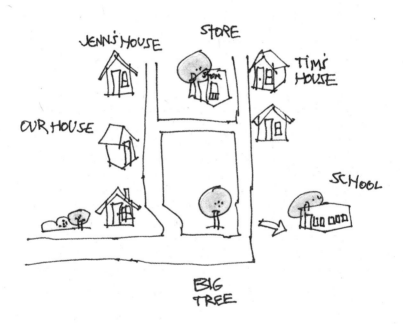

Learn How to Apologize

Learning to apologize goes along with learning to admit your mistakes. Sometimes when you make a mistake, like hurting someone's feelings or forgetting to do a chore or even accidentally running into them during a game, it's important to say you're sorry.

Seems simple, right? Just say, "I'm sorry." But you'd be surprised how many people have a really hard time apologizing to somebody else. To be honest, it can be a little humbling or even embarrassing to say you're sorry for something because in order to do so, you first have to admit you did something wrong—and nobody likes to admit that.

But if you want to have friends, chances are you'll need to apologize occasionally.

Sometimes, when you're tired or upset or someone is really bugging you, you end up saying something you're sorry for later. You might call them a name or tell them they're stupid or say something else that's not too cool. So, when you do that (and who doesn't?), wait a little bit till you're calmed down and then go to that person and say, "I'm sorry I called you that. I didn't mean it. That wasn't nice."

One thing you don't want to do when you apologize is say something like, "Sorry I called you a name, but you were driving me crazy and pushing me until I just couldn't take it anymore!" That's not really apologizing. That's just telling the other person what they did wrong *again*, and that doesn't really help.

Just say, "I'm sorry, will you forgive me?" and leave it at that.
After all, you don't want to lose a friend over some hurtful remark you just made. In fact, when you apologize to someone, sometimes it actually makes your friendship *stronger* because they realize you care enough about them to say you're sorry.

Learn How to Serve Others

One of the ways to have a great life is to look around. "What does that mean?" you ask. Well, it's a way of saying keep an eye out for someone you might be able to help. So often we live our lives looking inward and we end up caring only about ourselves. But God wants us to look outward and serve other people. There are lots of ways we can do this—from visiting a friend who's feeling sad to smiling at a kid as you walk by at school.

To be honest, sometimes it's hard to serve or even think about other people. After all, we've all got our own challenges, hurts, and fears going on. So how do you learn to "look around" and figure out ways to help other people?

One simple way is by keeping your room clean! Believe it or not, your mom or dad will love that one! You might do some chores around the house without being asked like taking out the trash or sweeping the sidewalk. You might help your little brother or sister learn how to shoot a basket or paint a picture or add up 4+7.

The first thing you should do is ask God for help. He knows it's not natural for most of us to go around helping other people. But guess what? He loves it when we do! Ask Him to help you. You might pray something like this:

Dear Lord, I'm worried about my reading test coming up later [or my swim meet this afternoon], but would you help me to look around and see if there's a way I can help somebody else?

Who knows? You might end up helping another kid study for his reading test. Or you might find a friend who's also nervous about the swim meet, and you can help her feel better and more confident.

As you get into the habit of helping others, it'll become more and more natural, and you'll have fun as you figure out new ways to serve others. Try it! You'll see!

Remember to keep your eyes open! Always try to be aware of ways you can do something for someone else. Here are some other great ways to be a helper to others:

1. After dinner, can you take some dishes into the kitchen and rinse them off? That's helpful! When you're at school, is there a way you can help the teacher? Can you pass out papers, erase the board, or put books back on the bookshelf? Can you open a door for someone who has their hands full? Always look for ways you can help someone out.

2. Can you read a book to your little brother or sister while your mom is busy? That's helpful! Why not teach a younger neighbor how to hit a softball or kick a soccer ball? You might have some toys you don't play with anymore. Think about donating them to a mission or daycare center for other kids to enjoy.

3. Help carry groceries in for your parents when they go to the store. Lend a hand when your mom or dad is making a meal. That's good for them, plus

you might learn how to cook something at the same time.

4. Speak nicely. Don't you love it when someone says something nice to you? Other people do too! Encourage someone with your words. You might say, "I really like the way you share when someone asks you." Or "That is a really cool backpack (or sweatshirt or hat)!" You might even say "You're the best. I'm sure glad we're friends."

The very best way to be a helper is to do it before anybody asks! It might take awhile, but as you learn to keep your eyes open and come up with creative ways to help, being a helper will become a really natural thing for you to do.

List five things you can do this week to help somebody else:

Try Something New

When you're a kid and just growing up, a lot of things are new. You'll make new friends, try new foods, and even learn new skills like crossing the monkey bars.

So, here's a bit of advice: Don't ever stop trying new things!

Sometimes as we get older, we begin to step back from trying new things. And we do that for a lot of different reasons.

One reason you might resist trying something new is that you are scared of the whole idea. Trying a new sport, for example, might be scary for you. The thought of learning something like skiing, snowboarding, or skateboarding might make you nervous.

That's okay. Some things might be a little scary, so make sure you've got someone who knows what they're doing and will keep you safe while they teach you how to do the new thing successfully.

Another reason you might not want to start something new is that you're afraid you'll fail at it.

Yeah, that's right, you might fail, but so what? Nobody's great at everything they do the very first time they try it. It's all right if you don't succeed the first time, just go at it again. Every time you try—whatever it is—you'll get better and better, and pretty soon you'll get really good at it.

And finally, you might not want to try something new because well, other people might be watching, and you might look silly.

This might be true, but one thing to remember is that most people aren't looking at you that much. Most of us just look at ourselves most of the time. But even if they are looking at you, so what? Way down deep they're probably impressed because at least you're trying something new!

And trying new things might include learning to play the guitar, making a video, or learning a different language. There are lots of new things out there to try!

So, don't let your fear keep you from trying something new. You might find an activity you'll end up loving!

Learn How to Ride a Bike

Riding a bike is a great way to get from one place to another, it's good exercise, and most of all it's fun! If you've never ridden a bike before, here are a few tips to help you get started:

1. First of all, you'll probably want an older person like your dad or mom or even an older sibling to help you learn how to do it.
2. Next, make sure you find a bike that's just right for your size. Getting a bike that's too big or too small will make learning much harder.
3. Always make sure you have a bike helmet. This is to protect your head in case you fall. In many states, it's the law to wear your helmet when you're riding. But

even if it isn't, it's *always* a good idea to wear one. When you first start out, it might be smart to wear long pants and maybe elbow pads and knee pads too.

4. Always practice your bike riding on a level surface and not in the street. A parking lot or your driveway are great places to practice. Keep an eye out for cars though.

5. When you're ready to go for it, get on the bike and check things out without moving. Just sit on it. Do you have hand brakes? Try squeezing them to get the feel for how they work. Make sure you can reach the pedals okay.

6. When you first start out, push off with your feet, and just coast for a little bit to get used to the feel of being on it. Don't even worry about the pedals at first. Get comfortable just coasting. Even if you only coast the first couple of tries, that's success!

7. When you feel comfortable, try pedaling your bike. You might have somebody hold on to the back and run with you at first. That will help you keep your balance. Believe it or not, the farther and faster you go, the easier it is to keep your balance. And if you fall, don't worry! That's a part of learning.

Just like everything else, the more you practice riding your bike, the better you'll become. Once you feel ready to ride on the street or sidewalk, make sure you learn all the traffic rules. See the following list.

Important Rules to Follow When You're Riding Your Bike

Always wear a helmet.

Ride on the right side of the street.

Obey all stop signs and traffic signals.

Be consistent. If you can, go in a straight line; don't swerve all over the street.

Find out if it's okay in your town to ride on the sidewalk.

Keep your eyes out for cars or other bike riders.

Let the people behind you know what you're doing. Always signal when you're about to turn. Here are a few signals to practice:

Right Turn

Left Turn

Slowing Down

DID YOU KNOW?

The average person eats 35,000 cookies in their lifetime.

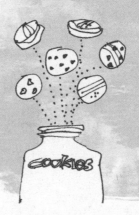

 # Stick with It!

It's really fun when you get what you want right away, isn't it? Like when you go to a fast-food place, and you get your food fast! (That's probably where they got the name *fast food* when you think about it.)

Or how about when you're learning to play volleyball or an instrument or learning how to write and it comes really easy for you? *Wow, this is so simple!* you say to yourself. It's a great feeling to pick something up fast, especially when it turns out to be easy for you.

But what if what you're trying to do takes a really long time? What if you can't get the volleyball over the net or your guitar playing doesn't sound too good? What if your letters aren't turning out the way you want?

What do you do? Well, you've got a choice.

You might say to yourself, *Wow this is hard. And it isn't fun anymore. I think I'll just stop. I'm not sure learning how to do this is really worth all the trouble.*

OR

You might decide to keep going! There's a word for that—it's called *perseverance*. Look at that! You just learned a new word! Perseverance or to persevere just means that you stick to whatever it is you're working on. You don't give up!

Learning perseverance (or sticking to it) is really important! When you think about it, every person who ever accomplished anything great had to stick to it.

Whether they were a scientist, an artist, a pro athlete, a musician, an astronaut, or the president, when things got hard and they were tempted to give up, they stuck to it. They kept learning and working and adjusting until they accomplished great things.

So, if you're learning something new and it's hard, don't give up! When you stick to it, you'll not only get a lot better but also be learning an important lesson: to continue on when things are hard. That's a great piece that God wants to place into your character.

# Learn How to Swim

If you don't know how to swim yet, now is the perfect time to learn! Learning to swim has a couple of great benefits.

First, once you've learned how to swim, you'll feel comfortable and safe around the water. Whether you're at the ocean, by a lake, or hanging out at a pool, you'll feel confident that you'll always know just what to do when you're in the water.

But the second reason you'll want to learn how to swim is this: It's FUN!

Getting in the water is a great way to cool down on a hot day, get some exercise, and even play some games with friends. Marco! Polo! If you don't know what that is, I'll tell you in a minute.

"How do you learn how to swim?" you might be asking. The very best way is to take swimming lessons from a pro. Have your parents check out your local YMCA or swim club. Most of them will offer swim lessons at a pretty good price.

Most lessons last an hour and meet maybe six or seven times. And there will probably be four to eight other kids in the class. And if, at the end of the sessions, you're still not feeling confident in the water, you can always take the class again or with a different instructor. The important thing is to go for it! Get in the water and have a blast!

MARCO POLO? This is a fun game that you can play with two or three friends. One of you is the hunter. They close their eyes, and the others move around in the pool. The hunter calls out,

"Marco!" And everyone else calls out, "Polo!" The hunter uses the location of their voices to try to tag one of them. If someone gets tagged, they become the hunter. You can play this game in either the shallow end where everyone can touch bottom or the deep end (but make sure everyone is a good swimmer).

PS: Make sure you know how to swim before you jump into any body of water—a swimming pool, lake, or ocean. And always go in the water only when there's an adult around.

Learn How to Accept Disappointment

Nobody likes to be disappointed, but it happens to all of us. You might not make the team you're trying out for. Your friend might be moving away, or you didn't get the birthday gift you were hoping for. Your own family might have to move, or you got left out of a fun activity that your friends were all doing. There are all kinds of disappointments we face as we grow up.

So, what do you do when you feel disappointed?

First, feel disappointed! This might sound simple, but when you miss out on a fun activity, lose a game, or weren't invited to a party, it's normal to feel disappointed. And even sad. That's okay. It might take awhile to get over the feeling.

So now, how do you deal with disappointment?

Talk to God about it. It's okay to let God know you're sad or even mad about what happened. Just let Him know how you're feeling and ask Him to help you deal with it.

Then, think about it. Is there something you can learn from this? This might come after a few days, but think about what happened. Whether you lost your basketball game or you didn't do well on a project for school, is there something you can do better next time? Practice your three-pointers or work harder on the assignment? Is there something you might have done differently? Being disappointed might turn out to be a good opportunity to learn something.

Finally, realize that things will get better. Right now, you might be really upset with what happened. But remember, even though it hurts now, it's not always going to be this way. Just because things didn't work out this time doesn't mean they won't be much better next time. Remember, God has good plans for you, and He'll make them happen.

Disappointment is no fun for anyone, but everyone goes through it at one time or another. And there are ways to deal with it.

1. Can you remember a time in the past when you were disappointed by something? What happened? Do you remember how you felt?

2. What are some things you can say to God when you go through disappointment?

3. What are some things you can do the next time something or someone disappoints you?

Make a Prayer List

"What's a prayer list?" you might ask. Just like it sounds, it's a list of things and *people* you're praying about. Making a list is a simple way to remember the stuff you want to share with God.

Did one of your friends hurt his arm on the playground? Add that to the list. Ask God to heal him and make it not hurt.

Is somebody you know sick or not feeling too good? You can add that prayer to the list too.

Do you have a friend or family member who's sad about something? Put them on the list.

And don't forget the good stuff too. Thank God for all the great things He's doing for you.

When you make a prayer list and set a time every day to pray for the things on your list, you'll be amazed at how God answers your prayers.

Of course, you don't have to have a list to pray for people. You can pray anytime you want, list or not. But when you make a list, you'll have a better chance of remembering the things you want to tell God about.

When you make your prayer list, divide it into two columns. On the left side, write what you're praying about—your parents, your friends, a test, or a big game coming up. You know, stuff like that.

Then on the right side—and here's the cool part—write down when God answers your prayer!

For example, let's say you're praying for your aunt who's sick with the flu. Put that in the left column. Then when she calls and says she's all better, write that down in the right-hand column.

When you do that, after a while, you'll have a cool record of all the times God has answered your prayers. And that way you'll remember how good He is and learn to trust Him more and more each day.

Still praying about something God hasn't answered yet? Don't worry! Just keep praying. Hopefully someday soon, you'll get to put the answer down in the "God answered" column!

 # Learn How to Deal with Temptation

"What is temptation?" you might ask. Temptation is having a desire to do something you know is wrong. You might be tempted to look at someone else's paper during a test at school. Or you might be tempted to take a cookie or a piece of candy when you've been told not to. You might even be tempted to lie about something because you think you'll get in trouble if you tell the truth.

Whew! There are all kinds of temptations!

Some of them are BIG like stealing money from someone, and some are small like picking on a younger kid (though it may not feel small to them!).

"So how do I handle temptation?" you ask. Here are a few suggestions:

1. First, ask God to help you stay away from temptation. He wants you to be successful even more than you do! You might pray something like this: *Dear Lord, you know when I'm around the little kids I'm tempted to be a bully. Please help me to be kind to them today.* And He will!

2. If you can, stay away from whatever is tempting you. The Bible says to flee, or run away from, temptation (see, for example, 1 Tim. 6:11), which means don't get into a situation where you might be tempted to do

something wrong. If you are tempted to take something that doesn't belong to you, stay away from it in the first place! Go into the other room.

3. Try the buddy system. Tell a good friend about the thing that's tempting you, and ask them to help you stand strong. Knowing that another person understands what you're dealing with makes things a lot easier.

4. If there's a person in your life who's leading you into temptation, stay away from them! If you find that hanging out with somebody always seems to get you into trouble, it might be a good idea to choose some other friends. Sometimes you just need to say no to a friendship that's not good for you.

93 Be Kind

Don't you love it when somebody is kind to you? It might be your mom or a grandma or grandpa. They might take you for ice cream or to the movies or for a walk in the park. Or maybe they just hang out and spend time with you.

Don't you like it when somebody tells you what they like about you? Or that they like your new haircut? Or they pick you first for their team?

That's being kind!

And if you want to have an awesome life and treat other people the way you'd like to be treated, try being kind. There are tons of ways to do it.

If somebody helps you at the store, say thank you. Wave at your neighbor, even if you don't know them that well. If a Sunday school teacher takes extra time to help you with your craft project, say thank you and give them a smile.

Tell somebody how much you love them. Take a little extra time to show a younger kid how to draw a pony or how to jump rope.

Open the door for somebody, or answer a friend kindly even if they're having a cranky day. When your friend strikes out at baseball, whisper to them, "No worries, you're a great player. You've got it next time." You know, stuff like that. That's being kind.

It doesn't take much, and there are lots of ways to be kind to other people. And here's a little tip for you to have a great life: If you're kind to others, almost all the time they'll be kind to you!

What are some ways you can be kind to your friends and family this week?

Don't Worry about the Future

Seems like there are lots of things to worry about: wars, being alone, what class I'll be in next year, losing friends, a big test next week, climate change! A lot of people, kids and adults alike, spend a lot of their time worrying about what's going to happen in the future.

Now there's nothing wrong with planning for your future (and studying for that big test next week), but God loves you so much He doesn't want you to *worry* about the future. In fact, every time we worry about the future, we're acting like God won't be there with us, even though He's with us today and has always been with us in the past.

Can you think of some times in the past when God helped you? Maybe He protected you during a storm or answered your prayers for a friend. He'll do the same thing for you next week, next month, and next year! He promises to always be with us if we ask Him.

So, here are a few tips to help you learn to stop worrying:

1. When you start to worry about something in the future, tell God about it. Let Him know what's bothering you, and ask Him to help you. He'll either change the circumstances so you won't have to face it, or He'll be there with you when you do. If you're new to this whole talking to God thing, just say, "Dear God, I'm a

little worried right now. Will You help me?" That's all you need to do. Easy, right?

2. Then, take a moment to remember how many times God has helped you in the past, sometimes when you didn't even know it or ask Him to. He's always been there for you and will be in the future.

3. Think about all the things you're thankful for.

4. Share what's worrying you with your mom or dad or a teacher or a Sunday school helper. Sometimes telling someone you trust about your worries can really help a lot because now someone is sharing the load with you.

 # Stay Safe Outdoors

There's nothing much better than playing outdoors, whether it's wintertime and you're making snow angels or summertime and you're swimming in the pool with your friends.

But the best way to have fun outdoors is to make sure you and your friends are doing things safely. Here are a few tips to help you do that and keep your outdoor activities fun:

Be Safe in (and Near) the Water!

The number one rule when you're playing around or in the water is to have a grown-up with you all the time! Even if you think you're an awesome swimmer, you always need to have an adult with you when you're near the water. Don't ever open a gate and go into a pool area unless you've got a grown-up with you.

If you're in a boat, kayak, or canoe, always wear a life jacket. Be safe around water.

Take a Hike!

When you go hiking, always stay on the trail and don't wander off. This is important because if you wander off the trail, you might run into some dangerous plants, snakes, or animals. Yikes! You also want to stay with the family or friends you're hiking with so you don't get lost.

Recognize Poison Oak and Poison Ivy

Most of the time when you're in a park or hiking on a trail, poison oak or poison ivy have been cleared away from paths. But it's still good to be able to spot them and stay away. You can learn what these plants look like by looking them up in a book or online. If you see them on the trail, stay away from them or you might be itching for the next several days!

Stay Away from Critters

If you see a strange animal when you're outside, whether it's a dog you don't know or a wild animal like a raccoon, deer, or fox, stay away from them. Even if they look cute and fun, don't approach them! They might be scared and could be dangerous. You can look but don't touch!

If you follow these rules and use common sense, you and your friends can have a great time outdoors!

Run from Evil

"Hey, I'm just a kid!" you might say. "What kind of evil will I run into?" Here are a few things that might come your way as you get older. If you decide now to stay away from them, you will be ahead of the game, and it will be easier to avoid them in the future.

Drugs and alcohol. When you're a little older, like in middle school, some of your friends might think it's cool to sneak alcohol or to experiment with drugs. But as fun or cool as it might sound to try some of this stuff, it always turns out bad. Both these things can be bad for your brain and even your body. So, the best thing to do is to stay away. Never start. Just say no thanks. And if you can, walk away. You'll be glad you did.

Stealing. It might seem kind of exciting to shoplift small things from stores or markets. But the more you do that, the easier it becomes, and pretty soon you'll end up having to pay in one way or another. You don't want to end up in kids' court for stealing a small pack of candy.

Lying. Earlier we talked about being honest and the reasons we sometimes lie. If you are always truthful, you'll avoid a lot of trouble and end up being a trusted friend.

Bullying. If you're tempted to pick on or harass kids who are younger or smaller than you, realize that's not good. It's not good for them, of course, but it's not good for you either. You don't want to become someone who loses friends because you bully other kids. If it's a problem for you, talk to a grown-up, and they can figure out ways to help you.

97 Stay Away from the Darkness

In order to have a great life, you should always stay away from the darkness. Not the actual darkness like nighttime, but things that aren't going to help you grow in your friendship with Jesus. These are things like fortune telling, Ouija boards, and tarot cards. For some people, these just seem like fun and interesting kinds of games, but God would say NO to getting involved with them.

It might seem innocent to have your fortune told at a fair or to read your daily horoscope or to play with a Ouija board with your friends. But God knows that these things—called the occult—aren't good for you and can easily lead you away from Him.

When we get involved with trying to know the future in these ways, we're actually trying to play God and control things that we're not really meant to control.

Even though it's tempting to want to explore the spiritual world, the Bible specifically tells us not to do that. When we do, there's a possibility we'll open ourselves up to supernatural forces that aren't from God; in fact, they're just the opposite. They're from demons.

The devil would love to fool you into thinking you're getting messages from God when, in fact, these are messages meant to hurt you. Whether it's a horoscope in the newspaper or online, playing with a Ouija board, or using tarot cards, the messages can be confusing or even untrue. God doesn't want that for you, so the best thing to do is to stay away from any of these things. You'll be glad you did. And if you're playing a game online or with friends and you get a sense it's not good for you, that might be God nudging you to walk away.

We might not know what the future has for us, but we can always trust that God has great things in store.

So, play it safe and stay away from the darkness.

And if you've already played around with any of the things mentioned, just tell God about it. Let Him know you're sorry and you won't do it again. He promises to forgive you and help you stay away from that stuff in the future.

 # Build Character

You might not be sure what building character is. Some people describe character as "what you're like when no one is watching."

Sometimes, it's easy to look good when you're at school or church. But at home you might be mean to your younger siblings. Or grumble when your mom asks you to do something. Or cheat at a game you're playing.

At school when nobody's looking, you might be sneaking a glance at another student's paper to get a better grade.

Nobody knows, you tell yourself, but *you* know.

It's hard, but one of the things that will pay off big time all through your life is to be the same person when you're alone as you are out in public.

That's character.

If you're having trouble doing this, no worries. Here are a couple things you can do to develop character:

1. *Ask for help.* Ask your mom or dad to help you act the same wherever you are. If you're having trouble with saying mean things to people or picking on somebody, let your parents know. They can help you learn to control those things.

2. *Ask God to help you.* He wants you to build character even more than you do. Just let Him know that you want to live a good life and develop good character, and He'll help you do that!

 # Be Reliable

One of the coolest things you can do as you grow up is to become a reliable person. "What does that mean?" you ask? Well, for one thing it means that when you say you're going to do something, you follow through and do it. If your mom asks you to feed the dog, make sure you do it. When a friend asks you to come over after school and you make plans to be there, make sure you do what you promised and hang out with them. When your teacher gives you work to do at home, make sure you do it and turn it in.

Have you ever been disappointed by someone who said they were going to do something with you but then forgot or made other plans? It doesn't feel very good, does it?

But if you're a reliable person, you're being thoughtful of other people and showing them that you care a lot about them. And if you're reliable in your work, people will begin to trust you and know they can depend on you.

Be reliable!

Being reliable or someone people can trust to follow through with things is an important part of who you are. Let's talk about ways you can be reliable and trustworthy.

1. Have you ever been disappointed by someone who didn't follow through on something? Did they say they'd help you and not show up? Did they make a playdate and it never happened? How did you feel?

2. What are some ways you can be reliable? To friends? To your parents? To your teacher? Can you think of other people you can be trustworthy with?

3. Why do you think it's important to be reliable and trustworthy?

 # Learn How to Say No Kindly

As you grow up, you're going to have lots of chances to say yes to lots of things. "Do you want to go to the park?" "Did you want some pancakes this morning?" "Want to go camping?" But there will also be times when you'll need to say no to something, even if it's a good thing! So, why do you have to say no? Especially if it's a good thing?

One reason might be you've got other plans with your family.

Or the timing doesn't work because that's when you have basketball practice.

Or maybe you need to do your chores, so you can't make other plans.

Or maybe you just might not want to do it. So how do you tell someone no in a kind and polite way? Here are some tips:

1. If your friend invites you for a sleepover or a weekend trip with their family, the first thing you should do is let them know you can't answer right away. You need to ask your parents if it's okay, of course. Plus, by asking for some time before you answer, you can decide if it's something you want to do or not. Often when we're asked to do something and we answer right off, we say, "Sure! That sounds great!" But later we realize we didn't really want to do it.

2. If you decide to say no, you might say something like this: "Thank you so much for asking me to go on your trip to the coast. I really appreciate you thinking of me, but I'm afraid I can't do it this time. But let's hang out when you get back." Don't lie or make up an excuse, just tell the truth and let them know how much you appreciate the offer.

3. Sometimes when you're young you feel like you need to say yes to everything anyone asks of you. But once you learn that your feelings and wants are important too, you'll see that you can make choices that better fit you.

4. Sometimes you might need to think of the other person first and do something as a way to serve them. But it's important to learn the difference between serving someone and just trying not to make waves. Remember, it's okay to say no sometimes.

When you get older, you might be asked to do something you know is wrong, like trying alcohol or drugs or cheating on a test. But if you learn to stand up for yourself and say no now, saying no in the future will come much easier.

 # Be Thankful for Your Body

Did you know that the Bible says you were *made in an amazing way*? And that what God did was *wonderful*? Check it out in Psalm 139:14. God doesn't make mistakes! Nowadays, kids receive all kinds of messages about their bodies, and almost all of them are untrue!

Some kids are convinced they're too fat.

Others feel like they're too skinny.

Others feel like they're too tall, and others are sure they're too short.

But guess what? God loves you just the way you are! Here are three things to know when you think about your body:

1. You are so much more than just how you look! You've got this wonderful personality. You're talented, and smart, and creative. And you've got skills in sports or art or schoolwork. Your body is important, but it's just a small part of who you really are.

2. Sometimes kids are surrounded by images of perfect bodies on TV, in ads, online, or on social media. And since very few people in the world have perfect bodies like the ones on the screens (what's a perfect body, anyway?), almost all of us feel bad about ourselves when we see them. That isn't good. And it's definitely not what God has for us.

3. Most of us have good, healthy bodies that work pretty well. And we can be thankful for that. We can breathe and walk and even kick a soccer ball. We can be thankful for these things.

Now, of course, if you're not happy with your body and you want to do something about it—eat healthier, get more exercise, or maybe try out for a sport—then go for it.

But remember, God created everything about you. Your hair color, how tall you are, and even your shoe size. And guess what? He's super pleased with how you turned out! And He should know.

Sandy Silverthorne has been writing and illustrating books for over thirty-five years, with nearly one million copies sold. He is the award-winning creator of the Great Bible Adventure children's series, several joke books for kids, *The Best Worst Dad Jokes*, and *Kids' Big Questions for God*. Sandy has worked as a cartoonist, author, illustrator, actor, pastor, speaker, and comedian. Apparently, it's hard for him to focus.

Connect with Sandy:

SandySilverthorneBooks.com

SandySilverthornesPage

Sandy Silverthorne